Grammar and Punctuation

Teacher's Guide

Notes and Copymasters for Introductory Book and Books 1–4

Louis Fidge

Published by Collins Educational
An imprint of HarperCollins*Publishers* Ltd
77-85 Fulham Palace Road
London W6 8JB

www.**Collins**Education.com
Online support for schools and colleges

© Louis Fidge 1997

First published 1997 as *Collins Primary Grammar and Punctuation*
This edition first published 2002

Reprinted   10 9 8 7 6 5 4 3 2 1

ISBN 0 00 713213 1

Louis Fidge asserts the moral right to be identified as the author of this work.

All rights reserved. No part of this publication may be reproduced, stored in a retrieval system, or transmitted in any form or by any other means, electronic, mechanical, photocopying, recording or otherwise, except for the pages marked *Focus on Grammar and Punctuation*, © Louis Fidge, HarperCollins*Publishers* 1997, without the prior permission of the Publisher.

British Library Cataloguing in Publication Data
A catalogue record for this book is available from the British Library.

Editors: Gill Munton and Mitzi Bales
Cover photograph: Corbis © Randy Faris

Printed by Martins the Printers Ltd, Berwick

You might also like to visit
www.**fireandwater**.com
The book lover's website

Contents

	page
Introduction	4
The components	6
Statutory guidance	7
The National Literacy Strategy	9
Using *Focus on Grammar and Punctuation*	14
Class Record Sheet	15
Individual Record Sheet	16
Teacher's notes and answers	
Introductory Book	17
Book 1	24
Book 2	34
Book 3	47
Book 4	62

Introduction

Aims

Collins Focus on Grammar and Punctuation is a carefully structured course for pupils aged 6 to 11. It has been designed to support schools in meeting the statutory curriculum requirements for teaching grammar and punctuation and the Sentence Level objectives of the National Literacy Strategy.
It will:
- develop children's ability to use language clearly, concisely and effectively
- help children use Standard English where appropriate
- provide children with the vocabulary they need to discuss, reflect on and understand grammar and punctuation.

Approach

The course builds on the rich and varied language experience which children have acquired naturally. From the moment their lives begin, children are actively involved in learning and using language, and unconsciously develop an understanding of its rules. From this base, the course:
- gives children an opportunity to learn about grammar and punctuation in a developmental way, ensuring the systematic introduction and consolidation of key skills
- has a simple structure allowing pupils easy access and providing them with a clear framework for learning
- progresses smoothly from level to level, giving pupils confidence in their growing understanding and competence
- contains clear instructional language and activities adapted to appropriate reading and interest levels
- provides opportunities to explore language in a variety of stimulating and interesting ways, ranging from the clearly structured and directed to the more open-ended and self-directed
- incorporates an integrated system for regular, ongoing assessment of skills and understanding.

Definitions

Grammar
For working purposes, grammar may be defined as the study of how sentences are structured and formed. It looks at how words work together and what rules of language prevail.

Punctuation
For working purposes, punctuation may be defined as the marks which help the reader make sense of what they are reading. These marks make writing easier to understand and provide signals to help read with expression.

Standard English
This is the form of English used in education, government and business. It is the kind of English used by people who are well-educated. It is widely used in writing and speech for public and formal purposes.

Dialect
This is the vocabulary and grammatical conventions belonging to a particular geographical area or way of life. (Standard English originally developed as one of many English dialects.)

Accent
This is a style of pronunciation belonging to a particular geographical area or way of life.

Standard English

Standard English is a sensitive area. It is sometimes difficult to disentangle it from issues of dialect and accent, status and class. Standard English has come to be accepted as the model form of written and spoken English most likely to be understood by most people. An important point is that, as the National Curriculum states, 'Standard English is not the same as Received Pronunciation and can be expressed in a variety of accents.' It also states that 'pupils should be given the opportunity to develop their understanding and use of Standard English'. This course provides just such an opportunity.

Overview of the course

Grammar

Throughout the course children are gradually introduced to grammatical concepts and vocabulary. These are:
- parts of speech (nouns, pronouns, verbs, adverbs, adjectives, conjunctions and prepositions)
- parts of a sentence (words, phrases and clauses)
- sentence structure (subject and predicate, simple and complex sentences).

Punctuation

Throughout the course children are gradually introduced to various conventions of punctuation and the important purpose punctuation serves in helping to read and interpret a text. These include:
- different types of word groupings to convey meaning (phrases, sentences, paragraphs)
- aids to expression (full stops, question marks, exclamation marks, commas, brackets, inverted commas)
- aids to word meanings (apostrophes to show possession and contractions, hyphens).

Also available from Collins

Focus on Comprehension

Focus on Writing

Focus on Word Work

Focus on Spelling

The components

The course books

The course consists of five pupil books for children aged 6 to 11. Each book, except the Introductory Book, is divided into 20 teaching units and two assessment units. The Introductory Book contains 13 teaching units and one assessment unit. All the double-page teaching units are structured in a similar way and will:
- facilitate planning
- provide differentiation
- make pages easily accessible to pupils.

The following sections appear in each unit:

Focus
This section:
- introduces the key objective being taught
- provides the essential vocabulary and terminology for discussion
- provides concise, clear definitions and explanations
- provides examples, always accompanied by pictorial support
- provides opportunity for whole-class teaching.

Practice
This section:
- provides activities which consolidate key points introduced in the focus
- provides activities intended for all the children in the class.

Making sure
This section:
- provides an extension or development of the main focus
- provides activities with a higher degree of difficulty.

Practise your punctuation
This section:
- provides practice of punctuation skills taught so far within the context of the focus
- provides opportunities for the ongoing assessment of punctuation
- revises the focus.

NB An interesting teaching point could be the difference in the spelling of **practice** (noun) and **practise** (verb) in the section headings.

The Teacher's Guide

The Teacher's Guide:
- sets *Focus on Grammar and Punctuation* in the context of UK statutory requirements
- sets the course in the context of the National Literacy Strategy and shows how it fits with Sentence Level objectives
- provides information on the aims, approach, and structure of the course and practical advice on organising and using it
- provides both individual and class record sheets (photocopiable)
- provides a detailed scope and sequence for each course book, background notes on each unit and answers.

Statutory guidance

Introduction

Language pervades every aspect of life. In schools it underpins the whole of the curriculum. It is therefore important for children to learn about grammar and how English works in order for them to use it effectively, concisely and correctly. The explicit and specific teaching of grammar and punctuation is a statutory requirement throughout the UK. *Focus on Grammar and Punctuation* has been developed on the basis of the statutory requirements. A summary of these follows.

England and Wales: English in the National Curriculum

This states that 'pupils should be taught to organise and structure sentences grammatically and to use accurate punctuation'.

The following are relevant statements from the Programmes of Study for Writing.

- Pupils should be given the opportunity to reflect on their use of language.
- Pupils should be given opportunities to develop their understanding of the grammar of complex sentences, including clauses and phrases.
- They should be taught how to use paragraphs, linking sentences together coherently.
- They should be taught to use the standard written forms of nouns, pronouns, verbs, adjectives, adverbs, prepositions, conjunctions and verb tenses.
- In punctuation, pupils should be taught to use punctuation marks correctly in their writing, including full stops, question and exclamation marks, commas, inverted commas, and apostrophes to mark possession.

Scotland: English 5–14 Guidelines

The following are relevant statements from the *Attainment Targets*.

Knowledge about language

Level B	Pupils will show that they know, understand and can use at least the following terms: **letter**, **word**, **capital**, **full stop**, **sentence**.
Level C	Pupils will show that they know, understand and can use at least the following terms: **noun**, **verb**, **comma**, **question mark**.
Level D	Pupils will show that they know, understand and can use at least the following terms: **vowel** and **consonant**; **adjective**, **adverb**, **pronoun** and **conjunction**; **masculine** and **feminine**; **singular** and **plural**; **tense**; **paragraph**.
Level E	Pupils will show that they know, understand and can use at least the following terms: **main point**; **subject**, **predicate**, **clause**; **apostrophe**; **punctuation**.

Punctuation and structure

Level B	Pupils will use capital letters and full stops correctly in more than one sentence, and use common linking words **and**, **but**, **then**, **so**, **that**.
Level C	Pupils will punctuate many sentences accurately, including simple use of commas and question marks; begin to use paragraphs to structure writing.
Level D	Pupils will punctuate most sentences accurately; achieve some variety in sentence structure; use paragraphs; and begin to indicate speech in some way where appropriate.
Level E	Pupils will construct, punctuate and link sentences of different lengths, and organise them in paragraphs in order to shape meaning.

Northern Ireland: English Programmes of Study and Attainment Targets

The following are relevant statements from the document.

- The pupils' mastery of correct usage, including grammar and orthographic conventions, should be developed.
- Pupils should learn to improve the expression, clarity, structure and impact of what they compose or record.
- Pupils should be adding to their understanding of the mechanisms of their own and others' writing and acquire the vocabulary to express that understanding.
- Pupils should be helped to understand those technical terms needed to describe the features of grammar in their writing.
- Pupils should be encouraged to write in Standard English, where appropriate.
- Pupils should have opportunities to develop increasing competence in the use of the full stop, comma, question mark, and exclamation mark; they should be introduced to the purpose and use of the apostrophe; they should be taught the function of the paragraph. They should learn how direct speech is set out and punctuated.
- Pupils should be taught how to use connectives and pronouns appropriately.

The National Literacy Strategy

The National Literacy Strategy states that 'grammar is not systematically taught in most primary schools, yet it is essential to the understanding of reading and writing'. It contends that 'an understanding of grammar is essential to progress in writing' and that pupils 'should also be taught to be more reflective about how language works in order to control it more effectively, particularly when writing'.

The explicit teaching of grammar and punctuation is one of the three main teaching strands defined in the National Literacy Strategy:

1 Word Level
Phonics, Spelling and Vocabulary.

2 Sentence Level
Grammar and Punctuation

3 Text Level
Comprehension and Composition

This course has been informed by the National Literacy Strategy's clearly structured objectives. The accompanying chart shows how the *Focus on Grammar and Punctuation* course fits with the Sentence Level objectives of the NLS.

Index to NLS Framework Requirements

NLS Sentence Level objectives	Where objectives are covered in *Focus on Grammar and Punctuation*		
Year 1	**Books**	**Units**	**Pages**
Write simple sentences	Introductory 1	1,7 1	4/5, 16/17 4/5
Recognise and use full stops, capital letters	Introductory 1 1 2 2 2 2 2 2	1 1 2 1 2 3 4 5 6	4/5 5 7 5 7 9 11 13 18
Use capital letters for personal pronouns and the start of sentences	Introductory 4	1,4 8	4/5, 10/11 18/19
Further use of capital letters	1 1 2	11 12 2	26/27 28/29 6/7
Use of question marks	Introductory 1 1	2, 13 5 16	6/7, 28/29 12/13 37

NLS Sentence Level objectives	Where objectives are covered in *Focus on Grammar and Punctuation*		
Year 2	Books	Units	Pages
Recognise and use commas and exclamation marks	Introductory 2 3	8,12 8 7	18/19, 26/27 18/19 16/17
Match verbs to nouns and pronouns	Introductory 1 1 2 3 3	10 3 18 6 11 16	22/23 9 44 14/15 26/27 36/37
Use correct tense of verbs	Introductory 1 1 2 2	5,11 13 18 7 9	12/13, 24/25 30/13 40/41 17 20/21
Identify speech marks (in reading)	Introductory 2	9 19	20/21 42/43
Use commas to separate items in list	Introductory 1	12 14	26/27 32/33
Write sentences with capital letters and full stops correctly used	Introductory 1 1 1	1,7 9 10 11	4/5, 16/17 21 23 27
Turn statements into questions using typical question words and adding question marks	Introductory 1 3	13 8 2	28/29 19 5

NLS Sentence Level objectives	Where objectives are covered in *Focus on Grammar and Punctuation*		
Year 3	Books	Units	Pages
Use the term *verb* and understand its function in sentences	Introductory 1 1 1 2 2 2 3	5,11 2 7 19 1 3 16 1	12/13, 24/25 6/7 16/17 42/43 4 8/9 36/37 4/5
Use tenses accurately	Introductory 1 2 3	11 13 9 3	24/25 30/31 20/21 8/9
Consolidate use of question and exclamation marks	Introductory 3 3	2,8.13 4 2	6/7, 18/19, 28/29 10/11 6/7
Use speech punctuation in writing with capital letters to mark start of direct speech	Introductory 2 3 4	9 19 9 9	20/21 42/43 20/21 20/21

NLS Sentence Level objectives	Where objectives are covered in *Focus on Grammar and Punctuation*		
Year 3 *continued*	Books	Units	Pages
Understand the term *speech marks*	Introductory	9	20/21
Use the term *adjective* and understand its function in sentences	1 1 1 1 2 2 2 3 3 4	4 9 16 19 1 5 13 1 13 1	10/11 20/21 36/37 42/43 4/5 12/13 30/31 4/5 30/31 4/5
Recognise the use of singular and plural forms	1 2 3 4	15 7 8 6	34 16/17 18/19 14/15
Use the terms *singular* and *plural*	1 2 3 4	15 7 8 6	34 16/17 18/19 14/15
Understand the term *collective noun*	3	8	19
Use the term *comma*	Introductory 1 3	12 14 7	26/27 32 16/17
Understand further uses of capitalisation (new lines in poetry)	1 4	5 8	13 18/19
Understand differences in use of verbs in 1st, 2nd, and 3rd person	2 3 4	3 16 18	8/9 36/37 41
Understand use of the pronoun and its function in sentences	2 3 3 4 4	11 10 13 1 7	26/27 22/23 30/31 4/5 16/17
Ensure grammatical agreement of pronouns and verbs (I am, we are)	3 4	16 18	37 41
Understand use of conjunctions	Introductory 1 2	6 4 12	14/15 38/39 28/29

NLS Sentence Level objectives	Where objectives are covered in *Focus on Grammar and Punctuation*		
Year 4	Books	Units	Pages
Understand the term *adverb* and its function in sentences	2 3 4 4 4	10 1 1 4 5	22/23 4/5 4/5 10/11 12/13

NLS Sentence Level objectives	Where objectives are covered in *Focus on Grammar and Punctuation*		
Year 4 *continued*	Books	Units	Pages
Understand use of paragraphs	3 4	15 15	34/35 34/35
Reinforce use of commas	Introductory 1 3	12 15 7	26/27 35 16/17
Reinforce use of adjectives	2 3 4 4	15 5 1 5	34/35 12/13 4/5 12/13
Revise work on verbs and investigate tenses	3 3	3 20	8/9 44/45
Understand the use of apostrophes to mark possession and contractions	2 3 4	17 12 16	38/39 28/29 36/37
Correct ordering of words	Introductory 1	7 20	16/17 45
Recognise how commas, connectives and full stops can be used effectively in writing	Introductory 1 3 3 3	1,6,12 20 7 17 20	4/5, 14/15, 26/27 45 17 39 45
Identify and respond to correct use of common punctuation marks		(see above)	
Understand the use of connectives (e.g. adverbs, conjunctions) to structure an argument	Introductory 2	6 13	14/15 31

NLS Sentence Level objectives	Where objectives are covered in *Focus on Grammar and Punctuation*		
Year 5	Books	Units	Pages
Understand the difference between direct and reported speech	3	19	42/43
Revise and extend verb work (including auxiliary verbs)	3 3 4 4	4 20 1 2	10/11 44/45 4/5 6/7
Identify imperative form in instructional writing and past tense in recounts and use when writing	3	2	7
Consolidate basic conventions of Standard English	3 4 4	1 17 18	4/5 38/39 40/41
Use punctuation effectively in longer and more complex sentences (including colon, etc.)	1	20	44/45
Construct sentences in different ways	2 2	4 20	11 44/45

NLS Sentence Level objectives	Where objectives are covered in *Focus on Grammar and Punctuation*		
Year 5 *continued*	**Books**	**Units**	**Pages**
Correct referral of pronouns within sentences	3 4 4	13 1 7	30/31 4/5 16/17
Understand the term *preposition* and its function in a sentence	1 2 3 4	10 14 17 1	22/23 32/33 38/39 4/5
Recognise clauses	3 4	18 12	40/41 28/29
Use connectives to link clauses within sentences	4	12	28/29

NLS Sentence Level objectives	Where objectives are covered in *Focus on Grammar and Punctuation*		
Year 6	**Books**	**Units**	**Pages**
Revise use of verbs and learn terms *active* and *passive*	4	3	8/9
Form complex sentences	4 4	13 20	30/31 44/45
Develop understanding of less common punctuation marks	4	14	32/33
Revise work on complex sentences	4	20	44/45

Using Focus on Grammar and Punctuation

Organisation

- *Focus on Grammar and Punctuation* may be used:
  - opportunistically, using specific units to complement other work being undertaken at Text Level
  - systematically, working through the units sequentially as part of Sentence Level work.
- Each book is designed to provide sufficient work for a year.
- Background notes for each unit are contained in the Teacher's Guide.
- The units assume teacher input, introducing and discussing the main focus, ensuring tasks are understood, generating discussion and offering appropriate support during the working of the activities.

Whole class

- The whole class may be introduced to the main concept and terminology of each unit together.
- The **Practice** section in each unit then provides work for the whole class.

Group and independent work

- The **Making Sure** section provides extension work of a slightly more difficult nature, allowing for further work in a group, in pairs or individually.

Plenary

- Activities may be reviewed together on completion to consider common mistakes and reinforce the unit's key objectives during these sessions. The **Practise your punctuation** section is ideal for this purpose.

Assessment and record keeping

- Each Pupil's Book includes two *Progress Tests* which review the children's understanding of the grammatical concepts, skills and vocabulary covered in the preceding ten units. These can be used to:
  - check that knowledge has been retained
  - identify areas that may need revisiting
  - provide information of individual progress
  - provide information for individual portfolios/records of achievement.
- Each unit contains a **Practise your punctuation** section, which provides a means for the ongoing assessment of punctuation skills introduced.
- The Teacher's Guide contains **Individual** and **Class Record Sheets**. These can be used to:
  - check on what each child has covered
  - monitor individual progress
  - give an overview of the progress of the class as a whole.

Focus on Grammar and Punctuation: *Class Record*

Book _____ Class _____ Year _____

Note: It is suggested that a brief indication of pupils' progress for each unit:
/ = attempted;   X = completed satisfactorily

Name	\multicolumn{22}{c}{Units}
	1	2	3	4	5	6	7	8	9	10	A	11	12	13	14	15	16	17	18	19	20	B

Focus on Grammar and Punctuation © Louis Fidge, HarperCollins*Publishers* 1997

Focus on Grammar and Punctuation: *Individual Record*

Name _____   Book _____ Class _____ Year _____

Unit	Comment	Date
1		
2		
3		
4		
5		
6		
7		
8		
9		
10		
Progress Test A		
11		
12		
13		
14		
15		
16		
17		
18		
19		
20		
Progress Test B		

Teacher's notes and answers

Introductory Book

Unit	Content
1	Capital Letters and Full Stops
2	Asking Questions
3	Nouns
4	Proper Nouns
5	Verbs
6	Joining Sentences
7	Writing Sentences
8	Exclamation Marks
9	Speech Marks
10	Matching Verbs with Nouns
11	More about Verbs (past tense)
12	Commas
13	More Questions
14	Progress Unit

Scope and sequence of skills

Unit	Title	Practice	Making sure	Practise your punctuation
1	**Capital Letters and Full Stops** Page 4	Putting in missing capital letters and full stops	Making up sentences about pictures	Copying story; putting in missing capital letters and full stops; writing own ending
2	**Asking Questions** Page 6	Putting in missing capital letters and question marks	Punctuating questions about a picture and composing questions	Punctuating sentences and questions
3	**Nouns** Page 8	Completing sentences with nouns	Writing nouns beginning with given letters from a picture cue	Punctuating sentences and identifying the nouns in them
4	**Proper Nouns** Page 10	Writing some names of well-known story characters	Writing names of days of week and months of year	Punctuating sentences containing proper nouns
5	**Verbs** Page 12	Making up sentences about pictures using verbs supplied	Matching up verbs with nouns to say how different animals move	Punctuating sentences and identifying the verbs in them
6	**Joining Sentences** Page 14	Joining pairs of sentences using **and**	Identifying joining words in sentences	Making up own ending for sentences containing joining words
7	**Writing Sentences** Page 16	Rearranging words to make sense in jumbled sentences	Rewriting sentences to make sense	Reordering words to make sentences and punctuating them
8	**Exclamation Marks** Page 18	Identifying sentences ending with exclamation marks	Punctuating sentences with full stops, question marks or exclamation marks	Punctuating a variety of sentences
9	**Speech Marks** Page 20	Writing dialogue given in speech bubbles as direct speech	Making up answers to questions in the context of a conversation, using speech marks	Punctuating sentences using speech marks

Introductory Book

Unit	Title	Practice	Making sure	Practise your punctuation
10	**Matching Verbs with Nouns** Page 22	Completing sentences using given verbs	Correcting verbs in sentences to ensure subject/verb agreement	Matching up beginnings and endings of sentences
11	**More about Verbs (past tense)** Page 24	Completing sentences using given verbs	Supplying own verbs to complete a given passage	Punctuating sentences and correcting verbs to agree with their subjects
12	**Commas** Page 26	Putting commas in given lists	Making up lists according to given themes	Punctuating sentences containing lists
13	**More Questions** Page 28	Matching up questions and answers	Changing given sentences into questions	Punctuating sentences and then turning them into questions
14	**Progress Unit** Page 30	Revising and testing of material in previous thirteen units		

Unit 1 Capital Letters and Full Stops

Focus
Introducing the idea that all sentences should begin with a capital letter and most end with a full stop.

Definition of terms used
A sentences is a group of words that makes sense on its own. A sentence starts with a capital letter. Most sentences end with a full stop.

Teacher's Notes
The concept of a sentence can be difficult to grasp. Full stops are peculiar to writing. There is no equivalent in speaking except, perhaps, for a short pause. Ensure that children appreciate the purpose of capital letters and full stops, which is that they give a signal to the reader, breaking the text up, telling the reader when to take a pause, thus helping to make sense of a piece of writing.
Some sentences end with a question mark or exclamation mark. These are explained later.

Answers
Practice
1. The farmer had some cows.
2. Clowns make us laugh.
3. Lemonade is fizzy.
4. Elephants have two tusks and a trunk.
5. Bluebells grown in the woods.
6. Children like to play marbles.

Making sure
(open)

Practise your punctuation
Two children went to the park. They took their dog. The dog chased some squirrels. The dog got lost. The children were worried. They did not know what to do.

Unit 2 Asking Questions

Focus
Introducing the idea of what a question is. Considers the punctuation of questions.

Definitions of terms used
A question is a special kind of sentence. We use a question when we want to know something. Whenever we write a sentence that is a question we must:
– start with a capital letter
– end with a question mark.

Teacher's Notes
Asking questions is a way of getting information. Invite the children to ask each other questions, for example, about their likes and dislikes.

Answers
Practice
1. When is your birthday?
2. Where do you live?
3. Who is your teacher?
4. What number comes before twenty?
5. Why do you go to school?
(open)

Making sure
1. What is Sam wearing?
2. Who is Sam with?
3. Where are the boys going?
4. How did they get to the shop?
5. What can they buy there?
6. When does the shop close?

Some suggested answers.
1. Sam is wearing a blue T-shirt, blue jeans and trainers.
2. Sam is with Asif.
3. The boys are going to the shop.
4. They rode their bikes to the shop.
5. They can buy things like pens and pencils in the shop.
6. The shop closes at 9 o'clock.
(open)

Introductory Book

Practise your punctuation
1. How many children are there in your class?
2. Who is your best friend?
3. The toy shop was shut.
4. Is it raining today?
5. Some children keep pets at home.
6. Do you have a favourite sport?

Unit 3 Nouns

Focus
Introducing the concept of nouns as naming things.

Definitions of terms used
A noun is a naming word. Nouns are the names of things.

Teacher's Notes
Ask children to point to things in the classroom and name them to reinforce the concept of a noun.

Hold a selection of things up and present children with some verbal cloze sentences, asking them to supply the missing noun each time. Use simple sentence structures like 'This is a _____' or 'Here is a _____' as in the Practice activity.

Answers
Practice
1. Here is a car.
2. This is an egg.
3. I can see a horse.
4. I can hear some birds.
5. These are socks.
6. Here are some apples.

Making sure
1. scissors, scales
2. books, brushes
3. ruler, recorder
4. dinosaur, door
5. clock, computer
6. paint, pencils

Practise your punctuation
1. A boy is writing in his book.
2. The teacher is sitting on a chair.
3. Some girls are painting a picture.
4. The mouse is in its cage.
5. The caretaker is mending the door.

Unit 4 Proper Nouns

Focus
Introducing the idea of proper nouns.

Definition of terms used
A proper noun is a special kind of noun. It is the name of a particular person, place or thing. Proper nouns always begin with capital letters.

Teacher's Notes
Remind children of the use of capital letters at the beginning of sentences. Reinforce the idea that capital letters also have a special use at the beginning of people's names and the names of particular places or things, for example, the names of the days of the week and months of the year. Look for examples of proper nouns in reading and information books.

Answers
Practice

Cinderella   Goldilocks   Paddington Bear
Little Boy Blue   Red Riding Hood   Jack

Making sure
1. Sunday, Monday, Tuesday, Wednesday, Thursday, Friday, Saturday
2. January, February, March, April, May, June
3. July, August, September, October, November, December

Practise your punctuation
1. Edward likes Wednesday best because he has art.
2. Emma had her birthday in July.
3. Does March come before October?
4. Shanaz lives in Brendon Avenue.
5. Is France bigger than Germany?
6. Mr and Mrs Grant went to Spain on holiday in July.

Unit 5 Verbs

Focus
Introducing the idea of verbs as doing words.

Definitions of terms used
A verb is a doing word. A verb tells us what someone is doing or what is happening.

Teacher's Notes
Mime some actions and ask children to guess what you are doing. Make a set of action cards. Each card should have a simple command on it such as sit, stand, hop, run, shout. Hold these up and show to individuals or groups one at a time for them to read and do as the card says.

Answers
Practice
1. The boy is reading.
2. The baby is crying.
3. The girl is jumping.
4. The dog is eating.
5. The cat is sleeping.
6. The bird is flying.

Making sure
1. Fish swim.
2. Birds fly.
3. Snakes slither.
4. Snails slide.
5. Mice scamper.
6. Elephants lumber.
7. Horses gallop.
8. Lions prowl.

Practise your punctuation
1. The frog splashed in the pond.
2. You cut paper with scissors.
3. Karen and Raza watched television.
4. Gary Gold plays his guitar well.
5. Mrs Green walked to the shops.
6. Mr Burton hums while he peels the potatoes.

Introductory Book

Unit 6   Joining Sentences

Focus
Introducing the idea of joining two simple sentences together by using some common conjunctions.

Teacher's Notes
Introduce the unit by discussing how we can join two pieces of string together by using a knot, and making one long piece of string. Explain that we can join two sentences by using joining words like **and** and **but** to make a longer sentence. Look for examples of the use of conjunctions **and** and **but** in reading books. Use the sentence in the unit to point out the slight changes that sometimes occur when two sentences are made into one. (Here the word **he** is missed out.) After completing the unit, encourage children to rewrite some longer sentences, which include the conjunctions covered in the unit, as two short sentences.

Answers
Practice
1. I went to the park and saw my friend.
2. Tess brushed her teeth and went to bed.
3. Humpty Dumpty sat on the wall and had a great fall.
4. Sarah has fair hair and blue eyes.
5. Mr Smart opened the shed and got out his garden fork.
6. The dog barked and chased the burglar.

Making sure
1. The door is shut <u>but</u> the window is open.
2. The road was busy <u>and</u> crowded with cars.
3. Ben ate some chocolate <u>before</u> he went home for lunch.
4. It rained <u>while</u> we were in school.
5. The mouse saw the cat <u>then</u> ran under the chair.
6. The sun shone brightly <u>until</u> it was time to go home.

Practise your punctuation
(open)

Unit 7   Writing Sentences

Focus
Introducing the idea that sentences will not make sense if words are in the wrong order. Reinforces the idea that sentences should make sense.

Definition of terms used
A sentence is a group of words that make sense. The words in a sentence must be in the correct order.

Teacher's Notes
Introduce the unit by giving children some silly sentences like 'The bones ate the dog' in which the meaning is altered by placing words in the wrong order. Ask children to correct them verbally and discuss how the meaning has been affected.

Write some simple statements on pieces of card, like 'It is a lovely day'. Cut up each statement into separate words and rearrange the words in the wrong order. Ask children to imagine that they have invented a speaking robot and have to programme it to speak correctly. Ask children to arrange the words of each statement so they make sense.

Answers
Practice
1. Dogs can bark.
2. Fish live in water.
3. My cat likes milk.
4. The horse runs fast.
5. A kangaroo likes hopping.

Making sure
1. The dog bit the postman.
2. The boy kicked the football.
3. The girl wore a blue dress.
4. The builder fell off the ladder.
5. The pop singer was playing a guitar.
6. The woman was watching television.
7. An old man cut the grass.
8. The children ate some crisps.

Practise your punctuation
1. My dog likes eating bones.
2. The sky is blue.
3. I like ice cream
4. It began to rain.
5. We are going to the park.

Unit 8   Exclamation Marks

Focus
Introducing the idea of exclamation marks.

Definition of terms used
An exclamation mark is a punctuation mark that comes at the end of a sentence. It shows the writer feels strongly about something. It can show surprise. It is sometimes used when giving commands.

Teacher's Notes
Find examples of exclamation marks in books. Read them to and with the children. Demonstrate the tone of voice used when expressing strong feelings about things. Say: 'This smells terrible!' 'What a lovely surprise!' 'Stop thief!'.

Answers
Practice
Be quiet!
This tastes delicious!
Put down that cat at once!
What a sensible child you are!

Making sure
I don't believe it!
I'm six years old now.
How tall are you?
Stop that this minute!
What time is it?
I really love reading!
I walked to school.

Practise your punctuation
1. The dragon chased the prince.
2. Has anyone seen my ruler?
3. It's not fair!
4. My book is on the table.
5. Thank goodness you've come!
6. Where is your house?

Introductory Book

Unit 9 Speech Marks

Focus
Introducing the idea that we use speech bubbles in pictures and speech marks in writing to show when someone is speaking.

Definition of terms used
Speech bubbles are like balloons that come out of people's mouths in drawings. They contain the words the person is saying.

Speech marks (or inverted commas) are used when writing to indicate a person is speaking. What the person says goes inside the speech marks.

Teacher's Notes
Children will have seen speech bubbles and speech marks in reading books and comics. They will probably have included dialogue in their own writing from time to time.

It is important that children begin to understand the conventions used in writing dialogue. A good way of introducing speech marks is through linking them with speech bubbles. This makes it easier to understand that everything the person says goes inside the speech marks.

To help children remember, explain that speech marks are like raised commas in the shape of 66 and 99.

Answers
Practice
1. Ahmed said, "I will put away the books."
2. Bami said, "I will tidy up the cupboard."
3. "I will clean the brushes," said James.
4. "I will feed the rabbit," said Lucy.

Making sure
(open)

Practise your punctuation
1. "Can you come out to play?" Colin asked.
2. "I cannot find my tie anywhere!" Mr Bentall shouted.
3. "Your tea is on the table," Mrs Carter said to her son.
4. "What a horrible day!" exclaimed Mr Shah.

Unit 10 Matching Verbs with Nouns

Focus
Introducing the idea that the verb in each sentence must agree with (match) the subject noun.

Definitions of terms used
A noun is a naming word. A verb is a doing word.

Teacher's Notes
This unit introduces subject/verb agreement in a simple way. Provide children with a number of sentences in which the subject noun and verb do not agree, for example, 'My hands is dirty'. Do this verbally. Ask children to listen carefully and identify what is wrong with each sentence. Write the sentences on the board and identify the noun and subject in each. Discuss the fact that in these sentences the nouns and verbs do not match (agree).

Answers
Practice
1. Cows moo.
2. Donkeys bray.
3. Horses neigh.
4. A lion roars.
5. Snakes hiss.
6. An elephant trumpets.

Making sure
1. The bells are ringing.
2. There is an apple in my bag.
3. Every day I walk to school.
4. The clock ticks loudly.
5. Aeroplanes land on the runway.
6. I draw with a pencil.
7. A bird is singing in the tree.
8. The children are running.

Practise your punctuation
1. A rocket is make of metal.
2. The monster scares me.
3. In the morning I get out of bed.
4. My cat chases birds.
5. I can ride a bike.
6. I need a new pair of trainers.

Unit 11 More about Verbs (past tense)

Focus
Introducing the idea that verbs may be written in the past tense, showing that something happened some time ago.

Definitions of terms used
A verb is a doing word. Sometimes a verb may be written in the past tense. This means it happened in the past (some time ago).

Teacher's Notes
Ask children to tell you some things they did yesterday, last weekend, in their holidays. Explain that these happened in the past. Write down some of the sentences. Underline the verbs. Explain that the verbs are written in the past tense to show the things happened some time ago.

Answers
Practice
1. On Monday Sita walked to school with Ben.
2. She took a packed lunch with her.
3. The class went on a trip.
4. The children travelled to the museum on a coach.
5. They saw lots of interesting things.
6. Afterwards, Sita felt very tired.

Making sure
(open – suggested answer)

Yesterday Hari and Lucy went for a walk in the woods. They heard a noise. They looked up and saw a squirrel in a tree. Nearby some rabbits were playing in the grass. The birds sang loudly all round them. In the afternoon, Hari and Lucy had a picnic. On the way home, they saw an owl. It swooped down to catch a mouse.

Practise your punctuation
1. On Monday I ran a race.
2. Yesterday Tom did four pages of writing.
3. Wesley caught the ball easily.
4. Last night everyone went to bed early.
5. When the man rang the bell, the dog barked loudly.
6. After Emma finished her tea, she played in the garden.

Introductory Book

Unit 12 Commas

Focus
Introducing the use of commas to separate items in a list.

Definitions of terms used
Punctuation marks help us to make sense of what we are reading. A comma tells us to pause. It is used to separate items in a list. In a list we do not use a comma before the word **and**.

Teacher's Notes
Explain that punctuation marks are like road signs to the reader. They tell you how to behave. A comma tells you to pause. To reinforce the use of commas in lists, play the game of 'In a (fridge) you would find (some yogurt, a bottle of milk, some eggs, a tub of margarine and a bag of tomatoes). Vary the game with: 'In a toolbox', 'in a toyshop', and such.

Answers
Practice
1. penguins, emus, ostriches, lions, elephants
2. red, blue, orange, yellow, green
3. a cat, a dog, two rabbits, five mice, two hamsters
4. curry, spaghetti, sausages, pizza, hamburgers
5. guitar, drums, trumpet, piano, tambourine

Making sure
1. (open)
2. A doctor needs bandages, a stethoscope, a thermometer and medicine.
   A diver needs goggles, flippers, a wet suit and a snorkle.

Practise your punctuation
1. In his bag Carlo has some sandwiches, some crisps, a packet of biscuits and an apple.
2. Out of the window Maureen could see two cars, a lorry, a bus and a bicycle.
3. The first months of the year are January, February, March and April.
4. My birthday presents were a ball, a book, a game and a watch.

Unit 13 More Questions

Focus
Extending the use of questions, introduced in Unit 2.

Definitions of terms used
A question is a special kind of sentence that we use when we want to know something. Whenever we write a sentence that is a question we must:
– start with a capital letter
– end with a question mark.

Teacher's Notes
Explain again that asking questions is a way of getting information. Discuss ways of framing questions, emphasising in particular the key question words (who, why, where, when, what, which, how). To elicit questions, select a busy picture and ask children to think of general and specific questions about it.

Answers
Practice
1. What colour is the sun? It is yellow.
2. When is your birthday? It is in June.
3. Where is London? London is in England.
4. What is your favourite drink? I like orange juice best.
5. Why are you so happy? I am happy because it is my birthday.

Making sure
(suggested answers as answers may vary)
1. How did the window get broken?
2. Why is the pencil blunt?
3. Who is at the door?
4. When was Tom's birthday?
5. Where is Paris?
6. Where was the cat stuck?
7. When will it be time for lunch?

Practise your punctuation
1. The racing car was red. What colour was the racing car?
2. Edinburgh is in Scotland. Where is Edinburgh?
3. In the morning the dragon came back. When did the dragon come back?
4. The meat cost five pounds. How much did the meal cost?
5. Mrs Martin looked out of her window. What did Mrs Martin look out of?

Progress Unit

1. a) Parrots are colourful birds.
   b) A lion can run fast.
   c) Does a giraffe have a long neck?
   d) How many legs has an octopus?
   e) Crocodiles like to sleep in the sun.
2. **nouns**: tree, girl, shop, house, crocodile, robot
   verbs: eats, climbs, talks, sits, swims, hops
3. a) April
   b) girl
   c) apple
   d) London
   e) Cardiff
   f) Wednesday
   g) garden
   h) river
   i) Queen Anne Street
   j) forest
   k) November
   l) boy
   m) Monday
   n) bird
   o) Pennington Road
4. a) Sharks have sharp teeth and live in the sea.
   b) You write with a pencil but paint with a brush.
   c) We came indoors when it started raining.
   d) The children shouted when they were in the playground.
5. a) Some cats are black.
   b) Aeroplanes fly in the sky.
   c) On a sunny day you can swim in the sea.
   d) We went to Spain for our holiday.
6. a) How far is it to the beach?
   b) What a lovely surprise to see you again!
   c) Put the box on the floor.
   d) Look out! There's a monster behind you!
7. a) "Where are you going?" Mark asked his mum.
   b) "I'm going to the shops," his mum replied.
   c) "May I come?" Mark said.
   d) "Yes you may, but hurry up," his mum called.
8. a) A kangaroo <u>hops</u> but snakes slide.
   b) Where <u>are</u> you going?
   c) Every day I <u>wake</u> up early.
   d) The gardener <u>is</u> digging up the weeds.
9. (suggested answers as answers may vary)
   a) Yesterday I went in the sea. It was very cold.
   b) Last week the greedy boy ate twelve bananas.
   c) Last night the wind howled and blew down a tree.
   d) It rained on the way home and Tom got wet.
10. a) My favourite colours are red, blue, green and yellow.
    b) Is art, maths, spelling or science your best lesson?
    c) When I come I will bring a bat, a ball, some swimming trunks and a towel.
    d) Amber's birthday is either on Monday, Tuesday, Wednesday or Thursday.

Book 1

Unit	Content
1	Writing Sentences
2	Verbs (1)
3	Nouns (1)
4	Adjectives (1)
5	Questions
6	**a** or **an**?
7	Verbs (2)
8	Nouns (2)
9	Adjectives (2)
10	Prepositions
	Progress Test A
11	Proper Nouns (1)
12	Proper Nouns (2)
13	Verb Tenses (past and present)
14	Using Commas (in lists)
15	Singular and Plural
16	Opposites (adjectives)
17	Conjunctions
18	Verbs (the verb **to be**)
19	Revision - Adjectives, Nouns, Verbs
20	Grammar and Punctuation
	Progress Test B

Scope and sequence of skills

Unit	Title	Practice	Making sure	Practise your punctuation
1	**Writing Sentences** Page 4	Identifying sentences	Matching sentence beginnings and endings	Capital letters, full stops; word order in sentences
2	**Verbs (1)** Page 6	Identifying verbs	Sentence completion using given verbs	Capital letters, full stops
3	**Nouns (1)** Page 8	Sentence completion using given nouns	Identifying nouns; classifying animals	Capital letters, full stops; constructing short sentences using nouns and verbs
4	**Adjectives (1)** Page 10	Identifying adjectives	Sentence completion using given adjectives	Capital letters, full stops; reinforcing work on adjectives
5	**Questions** Page 12	Matching questions and answers	Making up appropriate questions to accompany given pictures	Capital letters, full stops, question marks
6	**a or an?** Page 14	Selecting **a** or **an** to precede nouns	Selecting **a** or **an** to precede adjectives	Checking correct use of **a** or **an**; matching questions to answers
7	**Verbs (2)** Page 16	Selecting appropriate verbs to accompany a picture	Sentence completion using given verbs	Capital letters, full stops; selecting appropriate verbs to complete sentences
8	**Nouns (2)** Page 18	Sentence completion using given nouns; identifying nouns	Identifying the 'odd noun out'	Capital letters, full stops, question marks; writing answers to questions; reinforcing work on nouns

24

Book 1

Unit	Title	Practice	Making sure	Practise your punctuation
9	**Adjectives (2)** Page 20	Identifying adjectives	Sentence completion using given adjectives; composing adjective alphabet	Capital letters and full stops; composing endings for sentences; reinforcing work on adjectives
10	**Prepositions** Page 22	Identifying prepositions	Sentence completion using given prepositions	Capital letters, full stops; word order in sentences; reinforcing work on prepositions
	Progress Test A Page 24	Revising and testing aspects of grammar taught in previous ten units		
11	**Proper Nouns (1)** Page 26	Writing characters' names using capital letters	Writing autobiographical facts; making up names for pets; writing names of people and places	Capital letters, full stops, question marks; identifying proper nouns
12	**Proper Nouns (2)** Page 28	Sequencing a poem; writing days of the week	Writing months of the year in order; answering questions based on a poem	Capital letters, full stops; reinforcing work on proper nouns
13	**Verb Tenses (past and present)** Page 30	Identifying verbs in present tense; writing sentences in past tense	Sentence completion using given verbs in past and present tenses	Word spacing; identifying verbs in present and past tenses
14	**Using Commas (in lists)** Page 32	Punctuating sentences involving lists with commas	Making up sentences involving lists	Capital letters, full stops, question marks, commas
15	**Singular and Plural** Page 34	Completing regular plurals (just add **s**)	Plurals of words ending with **ch**, **sh**, **ss** and **x** (plurals require **es**)	Capital letters, full stops, question marks, commas; identifying singular and plural nouns
16	**Opposites (adjectives)** Page 36	Matching adjectives with opposite meanings	Sentence completion using adjectives with opposite meanings	Capital letters, full stops, question marks; identifying adjectives and replacing them with their opposites
17	**Conjunctions** Page 38	Joining pairs of sentences with **and**	Joining pairs of sentences with **but**	Composing endings for sentences involving conjunctions; identifying conjunctions
18	**Verbs (the verb to be)** Page 40	Sentence completion, selecting **is** or **are**, **was** or **were**	Sentence completion; subject/verb agreement (choosing correct form of noun to go with verb)	Capital letters, full stops
19	**Revision - Adjectives, Nouns, Verbs** Page 42	Sentence completion, choosing most appropriate noun/verb/adjective	Identifying nouns, verbs and adjectives; composing sentences to a given structure	Capital letters and full stops; composing beginnings or endings for sentences; reinforcing work on nouns, verbs and adjectives
20	**Grammar and Punctuation** Page 44	Composing and punctuating sentences based on given facts; identifying verbs	Word order in sentences; identifying verbs; changing telegraphic speech to sentences	Capital letters, full stops, commas
	Progress Test B Page 46	Revising and testing aspects of grammar taught in previous ten units		

25

Book 1

Unit 1 Writing Sentences

Focus
Introducing the concept of a sentence

Definitions of terms used
A sentence is a group of words that makes sense on its own. A sentence starts with a capital letter. Most sentences end with a full stop.

Teacher's notes
The concept of a sentence can be quite difficult to grasp. Full stops are peculiar to writing. There is really no equivalent in speaking, except, perhaps, for a short pause. Ensure that children appreciate the function of capital letters and full stops in the context of a sentence: they give a signal to the reader, breaking the text up and telling the reader when to take a pause, thus helping to make sense of a piece of writing.

Some sentences end with a question mark or an exclamation mark; these are taught later.

Answers
Practice
1. Most caterpillars are green.
2. A spider has eight legs.
3. Snails live in shells.
4. A fly has wings.
5. Worms live under the ground.

Making sure
1. A bird flies in the sky.
2. Frogs live in ponds.
3. A hedgehog has prickles.
4. Bats look like flying mice.
5. A tortoise moves very slowly.
6. Caterpillars change into butterflies.

Practise your punctuation
1. Wasps sting.
2. Ants are always busy.
3. Tadpoles grow into frogs.
4. A mouse has a long tail.
5. Bees make a buzzing noise.
6. Spiders catch insects in their webs.

Unit 2 Verbs (1)

Focus
Introducing the concept of verbs (denoting action)

Definitions of terms used
A verb is a word that describes actions. A verb tells us what someone is doing or what is happening.

Teacher's notes
This unit introduces verbs as 'doing' words. (At this stage, verbs as 'being' words are not introduced.) Only simple verbs are used, without any auxiliary verbs, for example: 'The farmer **drives** his tractor.' as opposed to 'The farmer **is driving** his tractor.'

A good way of drawing pupils' attention to verbs is to present simple texts with the verbs deleted (as in the 'Making sure' activity). This focuses on their function.

A further activity is to make a set of 'action' cards. Each card should carry a simple command such as 'sit', 'stand', 'hop', 'run', 'shout'. These may be shown to individuals or groups one at a time. By asking the children to perform actions, this activity confirms verbs as doing words.

Answers
Practice
1. The girl <u>dug</u> the garden.
2. She <u>planted</u> some seeds.
3. The girl <u>watered</u> the seeds.
4. The seeds <u>grew</u> into lovely flowers.
5. The girl <u>picked</u> the flowers.
6. She <u>gave</u> the flowers to her Gran.

Making sure
1. A farmer <u>works</u> on a farm.
2. A pilot <u>flies</u> aeroplanes.
3. A baker <u>sells</u> bread and cakes.
4. A secretary <u>types</u> letters.
5. A mountaineer <u>climbs</u> mountains.
6. A plumber <u>mends</u> burst pipes.

Practise your punctuation
1.   a) One day, a farmer was digging his field.
    b) It was hot work.
    c) Suddenly his spade hit something hard.
    d) The farmer dug faster.
    e) He found a small wooden box.
    f) The farmer opened the box.

2. (*open*)

Unit 3 Nouns (1)

Focus
Introducing the concept of nouns as naming words

Definitions of terms used
A noun is a naming word.

Teacher's notes
Look around the classroom and name things to reinforce the concept of a 'noun'.

A good way of drawing pupils' attention to nouns is to present simple texts with the nouns deleted (as in the 'Practice' activity). This focuses on their function. This could easily be done verbally.

A good way of checking whether a word is a noun or not is to apply a simple test. Try putting the indefinite article (**a** or **an**) or the definite article (**the**) in front of the word. Generally, if it is a noun it will take an article ('**the** ball' but not '**the** went'). Of course, this rule of thumb doesn't work in the case of a word which serves as different parts of speech depending on context. ('I wore a **ring**.' 'I **ring** the doorbell.)

Answers
Practice
1. I spread butter on my bread.
2. Ice cream is very cold.
3. I like to drink a glass of milk.
4. Strawberries and cream are lovely.
5. You can put cheese in a sandwich.

Making sure
1.   a) Hens lay eggs.
    b) Wool comes from a sheep.
    c) The horse ran out of the stable.
    d) The cat chased a mouse.

2. (*open*)

Practise your punctuation
1-2. Cows moo.
   Mice squeak.
   Cats mew.
   Horses neigh.
   Dogs bark.
   Birds sing.
   Sheep bleat.
   Donkeys bray.

Unit 4 Adjectives (1)

Focus
Introducing the concept of adjectives as describing words

Definitions of terms used
An adjective is a describing word. Adjectives tell us more about nouns.

Teacher's notes
Explain that adjectives are very useful words, giving us more information about nouns.

Pick up objects in the classroom and ask questions like 'What sort of a pencil is this?' Elicit a number of different responses from the children. Provide a structure for their responses, such as 'It is a _____ (long, short, sharp, red) pencil.' Have fun with adjectives and nouns: 'Horace was a _____ giant.' 'The dog was _____.'

Adjectives often precede the noun they are describing, but this does not always have to be the case, as in the last example.

Answers
Practice
1. Jack sold the brown cow.
2. He planted the magic beans.
3. Jack climbed the tall beanstalk.
4. Jack saw an old castle.
5. The giant was very fierce.
6. Jack stole the bag of gold coins.

Making sure
1 a) The bridge was wooden.
  b) The river was wide.
  c) The forest was dark.
2. (*open*)

Practise your punctuation
1-2 a) The funny clown had a red nose.
  b) He wore a yellow jacket and baggy trousers.
  c) The clown had long legs and big boots.
  d) His tall hat had a pink feather in it.

Unit 5 Questions

Focus
Introducing the concept of questions

Definitions of terms used
A question is a sentence that we use when we want to know something. Whenever we write a sentence that is a question we must:
- put a capital letter at the beginning
- put a question mark at the end.

Teacher's notes
Asking questions is a way of getting more information.

Book 1

Discuss ways of framing questions, emphasising the key 'question' words (**who**, **why**, **where**, **when**, **what**, **which**, **how**).

To elicit questions, select a 'busy' picture and ask children to think of general or specific questions they would like to ask about it. Sharpen the focus by asking children to think of questions they would like to ask a particular person in the picture, such as a firefighter.

Answers   *Practice*
1. What colour is grass? It is green.
2. Do you have a pet? I have a cat.
3. When is your birthday? It is in March.
4. Where is my book?   You left it in the bedroom.
5. Why are you so happy? It is my birthday.

Making sure
1-4. (*open*)

Practise your punctuation
What is pink?
I think a rose is pink.
What is red?
The hat on my head is red.
What is green?
Grass is green with flowers in between.
What is orange?
A lemon is yellow but an orange is orange.

Unit 6 a or an?

Focus
Introducing the indefinite articles **a** and **an**

Definitions of terms used
We use **an** in front of a word that begins with a vowel. There are five vowels: **a**, **e**, **i**, **o**, **u**.

We use **a** in front of a word that begins with a consonant. All letters that are not vowels are called consonants.

Teacher's notes
Revisit the work on nouns.

Name various objects that can be found in the classroom and practise putting **a** or **an** in front of each noun. Emphasise how you can check your answers by listening carefully and deciding whether they sound right.

Brainstorm and draw up a list of nouns that begin with each of the five vowels. Ask the children whether **a** or **an** should go in front of each. Discuss the fact that the use of **a** or **an** is relatively unspecific, whereas when we use **the** (the definite article), it refers to a specific object.

Answers
Practice
1. a pencil
2. a cake
3. an egg
4. an octopus
5. an insect
6. a snake

Making sure
1 a) an exciting (*open*)   e) a clever (*open*)
  b) a hot (*open*)   f) an interesting (*open*)
  c) an old (*open*)   g) a pretty (*open*)
  d) a long (*open*)   h) an amazing (*open*)
2. (*open*)

Book 1

Practise your punctuation

1-2 a) Riddle: Where does <u>a</u> baby ape sleep?
Answer: <u>A</u> baby ape sleeps in <u>an</u> apricot.
b) Riddle: What has hands and <u>a</u> face but no legs?
Answer: <u>A</u> clock has hands and <u>a</u> face but no legs.
c) Riddle: What gets wets as it dries?
Answer: <u>A</u> towel gets wet as it dries.

Unit 7 Verbs (2)

Focus
Introducing the idea that verbs may be made up of more than one word

Definitions of terms used
Sometimes verbs can be made up of more than one word.

Teacher's notes
In Unit 2, only simple one-word verbs were used. Although there is no need to introduce the term 'auxiliary verb' yet, it is important for children to understand that the main verb often has a 'helper' verb such as **is**.

Do the 'Practice' activity verbally first, asking children to frame their answers in sentence form. This will show them 'helper' verbs in action. Take the opportunity to reinforce the fact that many verbs are 'doing' words.

Answers
Practice

playing; singing/shouting; drinking; eating; dancing; jumping; laughing

Making sure
1. Tom is watching television.
2. Sam is looking out of the window.
3. The baby is eating her dinner.
4. The postman is delivering some letters.
5. The dog is barking at the postman.
6. Mrs Green is reading a newspaper.
7. The cat is drinking a bowl of milk.

Practise your punctuation

1-3. Each question has more than one possible answer. These are the most likely answers.
a) The footballer <u>kicked</u> the ball.
b) The baker <u>baked</u> some bread.
c) A boy <u>climbed</u> over the wall.
d) A pilot <u>flew</u> an aeroplane.
e) The girl <u>rode</u> her bike.

Unit 8 Nouns (2)

Focus
Developing the concept of nouns as naming words

Definitions of terms used
A noun is a naming word. A noun is the name of a person, place or thing.

Teacher's notes
This unit extends the definition of a noun. Revisit some of the suggested activities from Unit 3.

Brainstorm the names of as many different occupations as possible. When thinking about place names, ask children questions like 'Tell me the noun that is the name of a place where you can go and swim/pray/play/eat.' Take the opportunity to revise the work done on indefinite articles by asking children to use **a** or **an** in front of each noun suggested.

Answers
Practice

1. a) An <u>ant</u> lives in a <u>nest</u>.
   b) A <u>rabbit</u> lives in a <u>burrow</u>.
   c) A <u>bee</u> lives in a <u>hive</u>.
   d) A <u>horse</u> lives in a <u>stable</u>.
   e) A <u>snail</u> lives in a <u>shell</u>.
   f) A <u>spider</u> lives in a <u>web</u>.
   g) A <u>lion</u> lives in a <u>den</u>.
   h) A <u>pig</u> lives in a <u>sty</u>.

Making sure
1. horse sheep <u>bus</u> cow
   Bus is the odd one out. The others are all names of animals.
2. <u>apple</u> shoe boot trainer
   Apple is the odd one out. The others are all names of footwear.
3. potato <u>bicycle</u> carrot cabbage
   Bicycle is the odd one out. The others are all names of vegetables.
4. guitar trumpet piano <u>computer</u>
   Computer is the odd one out. The others are all names of musical instruments.
5. knife fork <u>plate</u> spoon
   Plate is the odd one out. The others are all names of things you eat with.
6. teacher dentist doctor <u>rabbit</u>
   Rabbit is the odd one out. The others are all types of job.

Practise your punctuation

1-3. (*open*)

Unit 9 Adjectives (2)

Focus
Developing the concept of adjectives as describing words

Definitions of terms used
Remember - an adjective is a describing word.

Teacher's notes
This unit builds on the work introduced in Unit 4.

Explain that adjectives are very useful words, giving more information about nouns and making writing much more interesting and informative.

Give a simple sentence such as 'The girl came into the room.' Identify the two nouns in the sentence (**girl** and **room**). Discuss how much more helpful it would be to have described the girl and the room in a little more detail: 'The tall girl came into the crowded room.' 'The untidy girl came into the noisy room.' 'The tired girl came into the smoky room.' Provide a few simple sentences and encourage the children to elaborate them in a similar way through discussion.

Answers
Practice

1. the <u>tall</u> giant
2. <u>shiny</u> apples
3. an <u>open</u> door
4. a <u>glass</u> slipper
5. a <u>long</u> nose
6. <u>fierce</u> dragons

Book 1

7. a <u>rich</u> king
8. an <u>angry</u> elf
9. a <u>sharp</u> needle

Making sure
1. a) Patch was a big, black cat.
   b) He had soft fur and a long tail.
   c) His eyes were green and bright.
   d) His ears were pointed.
   e) Patch had sharp claws on his paws.
2. *(open)*

Practise your punctuation
1-3. *(open)*

Unit 10 Prepositions

Focus
Introducing the concept of prepositions

Definitions of terms used
A preposition is a word that tells us the position of one thing in relation to another.

Teacher's notes
Look at the word **preposition**. Draw children's attention to the fact that it contains the word **position**. This will help them to remember the function of prepositions.
Demonstrate physically how prepositions work with objects in the classroom, using some of the prepositions introduced in the unit.

Answers
Practice
1. The lion is standing <u>by</u> the tree.
2. The mouse is <u>on</u> the chair.
3. The helicopter is <u>above</u> the house.
4. The squirrel jumped <u>off</u> the wall.
6. The crocodile went <u>into</u> the river.

Making sure
1. Each question has more than one possible answer. These are the most likely answers.
   a) The mouse ran into a hole.
   b) The wind blew the man's hat off his head.
   c) The silly boy ran across the road without looking.
   d) Youssef hid behind a tree.
   e) The burglar climbed over the fence.
   f) The train sped through the tunnel.
2. *(open)*

Practise your punctuation
1-3 a) A fox walked <u>through</u> a wood.
   b) A mouse ran <u>up</u> the clock.
   c) The money is <u>in</u> my pocket.
   d) Sam kicked the ball <u>over</u> the wall.
   e) Some treasure is hidden <u>under</u> the rock.

Progress Test A

Answers
1. a) The aeroplane is in the hangar.
   b) The aeroplane is above the helicopter.
   c) The aeroplane is below the clouds.
2. a) an ambulance
   b) a dinosaur
   c) a cake
   d) an orange
   e) a red pen
   f) a duck
3.
Things we wear	Things we read	Things we eat
sock	newspaper	cake
pants	book	eggs
jumper	comic	bread
coat	magazine	apple
4. *(open)*
5. a) The (crocodile) is crawling.
   b) The (frog) is hopping.
   c) The (eagle) is flying.
   d) The (shark) is swimming.
   e) The (koala) is climbing.
6. There are a number of alternative answers. Here is one version of the passage.
   Sam switched off the television. She gave her mum a kiss and patted the dog. Then Sam went upstairs. She took off her clothes and put on her nightdress. She washed her face and brushed her teeth. Sam got into bed and read a book. Soon she fell asleep.

Unit 11 Proper Nouns (1)

Focus
Introducing the concept of proper nouns

Definitions of terms used
A proper noun is the name of a particular person, place or thing. Notice that proper nouns always begin with capital letters.

Teacher's notes
Remind children of the use of capital letters to begin sentences. Reinforce the idea that capital letters are also used at the beginning of the names of particular people, places or things.
Find examples of authors' names and book titles. Look for proper nouns in reading and information books.

Answers
Practice
1. Emma
2. Ben
3. Mrs Patel
4. Mr Green
5. Snow White
6. Humpty Dumpty

Making sure
1-3. *(open)*

Practise your punctuation
1-2 a) Can you tell me the way to <u>London</u>?
   b) <u>Ben</u> and <u>Emma</u> come from <u>Dover</u>.
   c) The capital of <u>Wales</u> is <u>Cardiff</u>.
   d) Is <u>Edinburgh</u> a big city in <u>Scotland</u>?
   e) The toy shop was in <u>King Street</u>.
   f) <u>Mount Everest</u> is a very high mountain.

Unit 12 Proper Nouns (2)

Focus
Introducing proper nouns as the names of days, months and special times

Definitions of terms used
The names of days, months and special times are proper

29

Book 1

nouns. Remember that proper nouns always begin with capital letters.

Teacher's notes
Revisit the work covered in the previous unit.

Ask children to write the names of the days of the week in sequence, ensuring that a capital letter is used at the beginning of each. Make diaries or find other 'daily' poems (like the one on page 28) to consolidate the point. The months of the year can be treated in the same way.

Brainstorm and write down the names of religious festivals, pointing out the capital letter at the beginning of each.

Answers
Practice
Monday's child eats fish and chips.
Tuesday's child spits apple pips.
Wednesday's child eats beans on toast.
Thursday's child eats the most.
Friday's child is full of food.
Saturday's child is very rude.
But a child who is born on a Sunday
has sunshine for dinner every day.

Making sure
1. January, February, March, April, May, June, July, August, September, October, November, December
2. a) April, June, September and November have thirty days.
   b) January, March, May, July, August, October and December have thirty-one days.
   c) February is the shortest month.

Practise your punctuation
1. Christians celebrate Christmas in December.
2. Jews celebrate Hanukkah in December too.
3. Muslims celebrate Id in either February or March.
4. Hindus celebrate Diwali in either October or November.
5. Sikhs celebrate Baisakhi in April.
6. Buddhists celebrate Wesak in May or June.

Unit 13 Verb Tenses (past and present)

Focus
Introducing the concept of verb tenses (past and present)

Definitions of terms used
Sometimes verbs are written in the present tense. They tell us what is happening now.

Sometimes verbs are written in the past tense. They tell us what happened some time ago.

Teacher's notes
Remind children that many verbs are 'doing' words which describe action.

A good way of introducing the past tense is to ask children to recount what they did before they came to school. Focus on the verbs.

Perform a variety of actions in the classroom such as sitting down, hopping or clapping. Introduce each action by saying, for example, 'Now I am sitting down. Yesterday I _____ down.' Fill the gaps and discuss the different form each verb takes in the past tense.

A point of interest which might be pursued is that information books usually describe things in the present tense, whereas fiction books tend to be written in the past tense.

Answers
Practice
1-2 a) Ben is washing his face. Yesterday Ben washed his face.
   b) Ben is reading a book. Yesterday Ben read a book.
   c) Ben is watching television. Yesterday Ben watched television.
   d) Ben is climbing a tree. Yesterday Ben climbed a tree.
   e) Ben is painting a picture. Yesterday Ben painted a picture.
   f) Ben is kicking a ball. Yesterday Ben kicked a ball.

Making sure
1. Owls sleep during the day. At night they fly through the woods and hunt for food. Owls have sharp eyes. They eat small animals like mice.
2. Olly the owl sat on the branch of the tree. Slowly he looked all around. Suddenly he heard a noise. A mouse ran through the grass below. Olly flapped his wings and dived towards the mouse.

Practise your punctuation
1-2 a) The boy (jumped) up.
   b) Yesterday Sam (walked) to school.
   c) I am eating my dinner.
   d) Some children are shouting.

Unit 14 Using Commas (in lists)

Focus
Introducing the use of commas in sentences for separating items in a list

Definitions of terms used
Punctuation marks help us to make sense of what we are reading.

A full stop tells us to stop. We have come to the end of a sentence.

A question mark tells us that a question is being asked.

A comma tells us to pause. It is used to separate items in a list. In a list we do not use a comma before the word **and**.

Teacher's notes
The unit begins by reminding children of the punctuation marks encountered so far.

Talk to the children about road signs. They help the motorist to anticipate and to drive appropriately. In a similar way, punctuation marks are there to help the reader and to act as signals about how to behave.

Provide all the children with copies of the same passage. Ask them to follow it as you read it to them, deliberately ignoring the punctuation marks. Discuss their reactions. Discuss the various punctuation marks and the way in which they affect meaning and expression.

To reinforce the use of commas in lists, play the 'In a _____ you would find _____' game. For example: 'In a tool box you would find a hammer, a screwdriver, some nails and a drill.'

Answers
Practice
1. At the zoo we saw some penguins, emus, ostriches, lions and elephants.
2. In my bag I have a book, a pencil, a ruler, an apple and some crisps.

Book 1

3. Ali had a cat, a dog, two goldfish, a budgie and a gerbil.
4. Ruth has a round face, black hair, brown eyes, a small nose and freckles.

Making sure

1. a) A footballer needs a ball, some shorts, a pair of boots and a jersey.
   b) An astronaut needs a helmet, a radio, a computer and a spacesuit.
   c) A builder needs a hammer, a ladder, some nails and a screwdriver.
   d) A hairdresser needs a comb, some scissors, a mirror and some shampoo.
2. (*open*)

Practise your punctuation

1. Jane likes hamburgers, pizzas, spaghetti and curry.
2. Where did Jason get his hair cut?
3. On Tuesday Lee stayed at home.
4. On holiday Emma has visited France, Italy, Spain, Greece and Holland.
5. Did you see any zebras at the zoo?

Unit 15 Singular and Plural

Focus
Writing nouns in the singular and in the plural

Definitions of terms used
We can write nouns in the singular or the plural. **Singular** means 'just one'. **Plural** means 'more than one'.

Teacher's notes
Look for nouns in books, and decide whether they are singular or plural.

Compare regular plurals (just add **s**) with plurals which take **es**. Find and list more examples of each.

Answers
Practice

Singular	Plural
farmer	farmers
field	fields
gate	gates
cow	cows
rabbit	rabbits
cabbage	cabbages

Making sure

1. | **ch** words | **sh** words | **ss** words | **x** words |
   |---|---|---|---|
   | match | wish | kiss | fox |
   | bunch | dash | miss | six |
   | catch | brush | dress | box |

2. one match but lots of matches, one bunch but lots of bunches, one catch but lots of catches
   one wish but lots of wishes, one dash but lots of dashes, one brush but lots of brushes
   one kiss but lots of kisses, one miss but lots of misses, one dress but lots of dresses
   one fox but lots of foxes, one six but lots of sixes, one box but lots of boxes

Practise your punctuation

1-2 a) On the coach there were fifteen girls and twenty boys.
   b) Mrs Green had two trees and five bushes in her garden.
   c) Tom likes apples, oranges, pears and peaches.
   d) Have you seen my pencil and my ruler?

Unit 16 Opposites (adjectives)

Focus
Introducing the concept of opposites (in relation to adjectives)

Definitions of terms used
Opposites are words whose meanings are as different as possible from each other.

Teacher's notes
Introduce the concept of opposites by reciting nursery rhymes such as 'Jack Sprat', 'The Grand Old Duke of York' and 'Pease pudding hot'. Draw attention to the opposites.

Play the 'opposite game', in which you provide an adjective and children have to call out the opposite as quickly as possible. This often provides an opportunity for further discussion of words which may have more than one opposite. For example, the opposite of **big** could be **small**, **little** or **tiny**.

Answers
Practice

1. fat-thin, long-short, happy-sad, narrow-wide, wet-dry, soft-hard
2. heavy-light, far-near, big-small, weak-strong, noisy-quiet, fast-slow

Making sure

1. A mouse is small but an elephant is big.
2. A rock is hard but cotton wool is soft.
3. Ice is cold but the sun is hot.
4. A lemon is sour but sugar is sweet.

Practise your punctuation

1 a) Dan drew a straight line.
  b) Do you like sweet things?
  c) Ruth's skirt was dirty.
  d) Is my dinner hot?
  e) The sea was calm.
  f) Are zebras wild animals?

2 a) Dan drew a wobbly line.
  b) Do you like sour things?
  c) Ruth's skirt was clean.
  d) Is my dinner cold?
  e) The sea was rough.
  f) Are zebras tame animals?

Unit 17 Conjunctions

Focus
Introducing the concept of conjunctions

Definitions of terms used
A conjunction is a joining word. Conjunctions are sometimes called connectives.
We use a conjunction to join two sentences together to make one long sentence.

Teacher's notes
Introduce the unit by talking about the word **junction** in the context of two roads meeting. Explain that we can often join two sentences with a special word called a conjunction.

Look for examples of the use of the conjunctions **and** and **but** in reading books. Reverse the process by rewriting long sentences as two short sentences, omitting the conjunction. Notice the slight changes that may occur (words missed out or added) when two sentences are made into one (or *vice versa*).

31

Book 1

Answers

Practice
1. I went to the shop and bought a comic.
2. Tom put on his coat and went out to play.
3. The dog ran after the cat and barked loudly.
4. Megan has curly hair and brown eyes.
5. Ali picked up the kettle and filled it with water.

Making sure
1. The red door is shut but the green door is open.
2. The lorry was slow but the racing car was fast.
3. Sara's jeans were cheap but Shireen's jeans were expensive.
4. Mrs Slater's bag was heavy but Mrs Naik's bag was light.
5. Dean is good at maths but he is not good at spelling.

Practise your punctuation
1. (open)
2. a) (open) but (open)
   b) (open) and (open)
   c) (open) and (open)
   d) (open) but (open)
   e) (open) but (open)
   f) (open) and (open)

Unit 18 Verbs (the verb to be)

Focus
Introducing the verb **to be**

Definitions of terms used
The verb **to be** is the most common verb in the English language. We can use it on its own or we can use it as part of another verb.

We use **is** or **was** when we are talking about one thing or person. We use **are** or **were** when we are talking about more than one thing or person.

Teacher's notes
Look for examples of the verb **to be** in reading books. Is it being used as a 'helper' verb, or on its own?

Mistakes with the past tense of the verb **to be** (**is/are, was/were**) are common.

Answers

Practice
1. The cat is asleep.
2. The apples are red.
3. The children are going to school.
4. The horses were galloping.
5. The dog was very small.

Making sure
1. The cake is very small.
2. Some apples were red.
3. The spade was broken.
4. Baby dogs are called puppies
5. The boy was reading a comic.
6. The girls were listening to the teacher.
7. The doctor is sitting in her office.
8. The kittens are playing with the wool.

Practise your punctuation
1. Katie and Harry were paddling in the water.
2. Two children were climbing on the roof of the shed.
3. The rain is pouring down.
4. The men are getting very wet.
5. Mrs Jones was waving to her friend.
6. The thief is getting away.

Unit 19 Revision - Adjectives, Nouns, Verbs

Focus
Revising adjectives, nouns and verbs

Definitions of terms used
An adjective is a describing word. It tells us more about a noun.

A noun is a naming word. It can be the name of a person, place or thing.

A verb is a doing word. Every sentence must have a verb.

Teacher's notes
Back up the work in this unit by looking for more examples of each part of speech in the children's reading books.

Answers

Practice
1. a) A frog hops.
   b) cow moos.
   c) A snake hisses.
   d) A bird flies.
2. a) A snail slides.
   b) Kangaroos jump.
   c) A fish is swimming.
   d) Some dogs were barking.
3. a) I had a cold drink.
   b) My suitcase was very heavy.
   c) The lemon tasted sour.
   d) It was a windy night.

Making sure
1. a) The ~~red~~ car sped up the ~~hill~~.
   b) ~~Tom~~ felt frightened.
   c) ~~Kim~~ wore a large hat.
   d) The ~~bike~~ had a ~~flat~~ ~~tyre~~.
2. (open)

Practise your punctuation
1-2. (open)

Unit 20 Grammar and Punctuation

Focus
Developing a deeper understanding of grammar and punctuation

Definitions of terms used
Grammar is the study of the way in which we make sentences. It looks at how words work together. It is to do with the rules of language.

Punctuation helps us to make sense of what we read. Punctuation marks make writing easier to understand. They help us to read with expression.

Teacher's notes
This unit revises and reinforces the understanding built up during the course of the book and brings together many of the teaching points, particularly in the area of punctuation.

Book 1

Answers
Practice
(open)
Making sure
1. a) Some aliens <u>wanted</u> a new home.
   b) The aliens <u>built</u> a huge rocket
   c) They <u>got ready</u> for a long journey.
   d) The rocket <u>blasted</u> off into space.
   e) It <u>landed</u> with a crash when something <u>went</u> wrong.
2. There are several different ways of expanding the telegraphic speech of the alien. Here is one possible answer.

We have come a long way in our rocket. Its engine does not work. Why are you frightened? I want to be your friend. Where do you live? Take me home to meet your family.

Practise your punctuation
The alien had a big, round body. It had a square head. Its three green eyes flashed on and off. Its teeth were sharp and pointed. The monster spoke in a deep voice with a booming sound. It bounced along on a huge spring which had a large, hairy foot at the end of it.

Progress Test B
Answers
1. a) I am a cow.
   b) I am a bat. (other answers are possible)
   c) I am a mirror.
2. Each question has more than one possible answer. Here are the most likely answers.
   a) Ice is cold.
   b) A wheel is round.
   c) A needle is sharp.
   d) The lions were fierce.
   e) A giant is tall.
   f) The teacher was pleased.
3. a) Puppies are cute.
   b) Baby cows are called calves.
   c) Some children are shouting.
   d) The chicken is clucking.
4. a) The bus was late.
   b) The boys were scared.
   c) Some cows were mooing.
   d) The cat was sitting by the fire.
5.
Singular	Plural
fox	foxes
cup	cups
stitch	stitches
jumper	jumpers
wish	wishes
pencil	pencils
boss	bosses
bird	birds
box	boxes
hutch	hutches
6. a) night
   b) girl
   c) winter
   d) answer
   e) enemy
7. a) open
   b) walk
   c) start
   d) sink
   e) shout
8. a) low
   b) hot
   c) soft
   d) smooth
   e) far
9. a) I ate a sandwich and then drank a cup of tea.
   b) Tom is right but Dan is wrong.
   c) Amy lost but Yasmin won.
   d) Mrs Shah opened the door and walked in the room.
10. a) Emma <u>is playing</u> hopscotch.
    b) The clouds <u>are</u> grey.
    c) The children <u>are shopping</u>.
    d) Every window <u>is</u> broken.
    e) I <u>am painting</u> a picture.
    f) We <u>are eating</u> some crisps.
11. a) Emma was playing (played) hopscotch.
    b) The clouds were grey.
    c) The children were shopping.
    d) Every window was broken.
    e) I was painting (painted) a picture.
    f) We were eating (ate) some crisps.
12. a) Next Tuesday it will be Tom's birthday.
    b) Christmas is always in December.
    c) Does the River Thames flow through London?
    d) France, Italy, Spain and Austria are all countries in Europe.
13. a) A sentence is a group of words that makes sense on its own.
    b) A verb is a doing word.
    c) A noun is a naming word.
    d) An adjective is a describing word.
    e) A preposition is a word that tells you the position of one thing in relation to another.
    f) A conjunction is a joining word.

Book 2

Unit	Content
1	Parts of Speech (nouns, verbs and adjectives)
2	Common and Proper Nouns
3	Verbs ('doing' and 'being' words)
4	Sentences and Phrases
5	Adjectives
6	Subjects and Verbs
7	Singular and Plural
8	Exclamation Marks
9	Verb Tenses (past and present)
10	Adverbs
	Progress Test A
11	Pronouns
12	Conjunctions
13	More about Adjectives
14	Prepositions
15	Adjectives (comparatives and superlatives)
16	Opposites (verbs)
17	Apostrophes (contractions)
18	Sentences (subject and predicate)
19	Direct Speech
20	Positive and Negative Sentences
	Progress Test B

Scope and sequence of skills

Unit	Title	Practice	Making sure	Practise your punctuation
1	**Parts of Speech (nouns, verbs and adjectives)** Page 4	Sentence completion using given verbs	Completing phrases with suitable nouns and adjectives	Capital letters, full stops, commas, question marks; reinforcing work on parts of speech
2	**Common and Proper Nouns** Page 6	Sorting and classifying common and proper nouns	Identifying common and proper nouns; compiling an alphabetical list of names and countries	Capital letters, full stops, commas, question marks; identifying common and proper nouns
3	**Verbs ('doing' and 'being' words)** Page 8	Identifying 'doing' verbs; sentence completion, using 'being' verbs	Sentence completion ('doing' verbs); identifying 'being' verbs	Capital letters, full stops; identifying 'doing' and 'being' verbs
4	**Sentences and Phrases** Page 10	Identifying sentences and phrases; locating verbs in sentences	Sentence completion using given phrases; composing sentences including given phrases	Changing the verbs in given sentences to make sense
5	**Adjectives** Page 12	Sentence completion, selecting from given adjectives	Identifying adjectives; supplying adjectives to improve sentences	Capital letters and full stops; replacing the adjective **nice**
6	**Subjects and Verbs** Page 14	Identifying subjects and verbs	Supplying subjects to complete sentences; supplying sentence endings to go with given subjects; identifying verbs	Capital letters, full stops; matching subjects with sentence endings
7	**Singular and Plural** Page 16	Completing regular plurals and those ending with a consonant + **y**	Changing singular nouns into plural nouns (and *vice versa*); subject/verb agreement	Capital letters, commas, full stops; subject/verb agreement; identifying plural nouns

Book 2

Unit	Title	Practice	Making sure	Practise your punctuation
8	**Exclamation Marks** Page 18	Classifying sentences as exclamations and questions	Supplying exclamations to match given pictures	Capital letters, question marks, exclamation marks
9	**Verb Tenses (past and present)** Page 20	Identifying verb tenses	Composing sentences using the present and past tenses; completing a chart of verb tenses	Capital letters, full stops; identifying verbs; changing verb tenses
10	**Adverbs** Page 22	Sentence completion using given adverbs; identifying adverbs	Forming adverbs from adjectives; supplying adverbs to go with verbs	Capital letters, commas, exclamation marks, full stops; identifying adverbs
	Progress Test A Page 24	Revising and testing aspects of grammar taught in previous ten units		
11	**Pronouns** Page 26	Sentence completion using given pronouns	Supplying suitable pronouns	Full stops, capital letters, commas; identifying pronouns
12	**Conjunctions** Page 28	Joining pairs of sentences with **and** or **but**	Joining pairs of sentences with **because** or **so**; identifying conjunctions	Capital letters, full stops; joining sentences
13	**More about Adjectives** Page 30	Supplying suitable colour, number and order adjectives	Supplying sentence endings; ordering adjectives according to degree	Full stops, commas, question marks, exclamation marks; identifying adjectives
14	**Prepositions** Page 32	Sentence completion using given prepositions	Supplying suitable prepositions to complete sentences	Full stops, capital letters; matching sentence beginnings and endings; identifying prepositions.
15	**Adjectives (comparatives and superlatives)** Page 34	Completing chart of regular comparative and superlative adjectives	Supplying comparative and superlative forms of irregular adjectives; sentence completion	Capital letters, commas, full stops; identifying comparative and superlative adjectives
16	**Opposites (verbs)** Page 36	Forming opposites of verbs by adding the prefix **un**; forming opposites of verbs in sentences	Forming opposites of verbs by adding the prefix **dis**; forming opposites of verbs in sentences	Capital letters, full stops, commas, question marks; identifying verbs; forming opposites of verbs
17	**Apostrophes (contractions)** Page 38	Writing contractions out in full; matching contractions with complete words	Writing contractions in sentences	Capital letters, full stops, question marks, exclamation marks, apostrophes; identifying contractions
18	**Sentences (subject and predicate)** Page 40	Matching subjects with predicates	Identifying subjects, predicates and verbs	Capital letters, full stops; changing the subjects of sentences
19	**Direct Speech** Page 42	Punctuating direct speech with inverted commas	Suggesting appropriate dialogue for pictures; using inverted commas	Capital letters, full stops, commas, question marks, apostrophes, exclamation marks, inverted commas
20	**Positive and Negative Sentences** Page 44	Identifying positive and negative sentences; changing positive sentences into negative sentences and *vice versa*	Changing positive sentences into negative sentences and *vice versa*	Capital letters, full stops, apostrophes; changing negative sentences into positive sentences
	Progress Test B Page 46	Revising and testing aspects of grammar taught in previous ten units		

Book 2

Unit 1 Parts of Speech (nouns, verbs and adjectives)

Focus
Introducing the concept of parts of speech; revising work on nouns, verbs and adjectives

Definitions of terms used
Grammar is the study of the way in which we use words to make sentences. Words may be divided into different groups called parts of speech. Three important parts of speech are nouns, verbs and adjectives.

An adjective is a describing word. Adjectives tell us more about nouns.

A noun is a naming word. A noun can be the name of a person, place or thing.

Most verbs are words that describe actions.

Teacher's notes
Words may be divided into groups according to their function (the way in which they are used in sentences). Parts of speech are sometimes called 'word classes'.

There are eight main parts of speech in English: nouns, adjectives, verbs, adverbs, prepositions, conjunctions, pronouns and articles. The term 'parts of speech' is slightly deceptive because these word groups are found in writing as well as in speech.

Answers
Practice
1. The old turtle crawled up the hill.
2. The porter carried the suitcases to our hotel room.
3. Mr Blake planted some seeds in his garden.
4. The secretary typed lots of letters.
5. Emma shouted at the top of her voice.
6. We sailed our boat out to sea.
7. The bull chased the children across the field.
8. The eagle carried the animal in its claws.

Making sure
1-2. (*open*)

Practise your punctuation

1-2 a) The frightened child approached the dark castle.
              a   n   v   a   n
                       v   a   n
b) What made that funny noise?
      a   n   v   a   n   n
c) The small boy was carrying a big bag, a book, a
      a   n   n
pointed stick and an apple.
      a   n   v   v
d) The old door creaked and opened.
    a   a   n   v   n
e) A strange old lady stood in the shadows.

Unit 2 Common and Proper Nouns

Focus
Introducing the concept of common nouns; revising proper nouns

Definitions of terms used
A noun is the name of a person, place or thing.

Common (or ordinary) nouns are the names of people, places or things in general. A proper noun is the name of a particular person, place or thing.

A common noun starts with a small letter. A proper noun starts with a capital letter.

Teacher's notes
Look for nouns in books and newspapers, and discuss whether they are common or proper nouns. Common nouns can be preceded by the definite article **the**, or by the indefinite article **a** or **an**. This is not the case with proper nouns.

Answers
Practice
Proper nouns
Snow White
Fluff
Manchester
Mr Barnes
River Thames
The Times
Mars
Sunday
Easter
Nasir

Common nouns
crocodile
bus
letter
house
shop
day
pet
word
woman
sentence

Making sure
1. a) The coach to Birmingham was full.
   b) At Diwali some people have a party.
   c) The boat sailed down the River Severn.
   d) During his holiday Ben visited Portugal.
   e) Sir Francis Drake was a famous explorer.
   f) My favourite team is Chelsea.
   g) Mrs Rossetti is a keen gardener.
   h) The book was The Pink Pyjamas by Barbara Miller.
2. (*open*)

Practise your punctuation
1-2 a) Ann Moore lives in Edinburgh.
    b) My address is 14 King Street.
    c) Have you ever been to America, Canada, Mexico or Jamaica?
    d) The mountaineer climbed Mount Everest.
    e) Is Christmas in November or December?

Unit 3 Verbs ('doing' and 'being' words)

Focus
Revising verbs as 'doing' words; introducing verbs as 'being' words

Definitions of terms used
Most verbs are words that describe actions. They tell us what someone is doing or what is happening.

Some verbs are 'being' words.

Teacher's notes
Remind the children that every sentence must contain at least one verb. Verbs can describe action ('doing' words), or they can be 'being' words.

Some verbs are made up of two words: the main verb and a 'helper' (auxiliary) verb: 'I **am running**.' When using the verb **to be**, children need to be careful to make the subject and the verb agree.

Look for examples of 'doing' and 'being' verbs, and for examples of auxiliary verbs.

Answers
Practice
1. a) Tadpoles <u>nibble</u> weeds.
   b) Tadpoles <u>swish</u> their tails.
   c) The frog <u>jumped</u> on to a rock.
   d) The frog <u>croaked</u> loudly.
2. a) Tadpoles <u>are</u> baby frogs.
   b) I <u>am</u> hot.
   c) Victoria <u>was</u> Queen of Britain.
   d) Ali <u>is</u> good at spelling.
   e) Tomorrow we <u>will be</u> one day older.
   f) The Egyptians <u>were</u> inventive people.

Making sure
1. a) If you throw the ball I will catch it.
   b) Cork floats on water but metal sinks.
   c) A customer buys things but a shopkeeper sells them.
   d) A captain leads and the team follows.
   e) The child lifted the heavy weight and then dropped it.
   f) The woman dug a hole and then filled it in again.
2. a) Samir <u>is</u> a tall boy.
   b) The doctor <u>was</u> late.
   c) Tomorrow <u>will be</u> Sunday.
   d) The Vikings <u>were</u> good fighters.
   e) How <u>are</u> you today?
   f) I <u>am</u> tired.

Practise your punctuation
1-2. Sooty <u>looked</u> up at the table hungrily. The budgerigar was in its cage on the table. The cat <u>jumped</u> up. The bird (was) frightened. Mrs Sharp <u>heard</u> all the noise and <u>ran</u> into (the room). She was very angry with the cat.

Unit 4 Sentences and Phrases
Focus
Revising work on sentences; introducing the concept of phrases

Definitions of terms used
A sentence is a group of words that makes sense on its own. Every sentence must contain a verb.

A phrase is a group of words that does not make sense on its own. Phrases are usually short. Most phrases do not contain verbs.

Teacher's notes
It is sufficient at this stage for children to understand the differences between sentences and phrases as defined in the unit. Later on, they will learn that there are different sorts of phrase (adjectival, adverbial and noun phrases).

One good activity to accompany this unit is to have a 'bag of phrases' containing slips of paper each with a different phrase written on it. The children have to pull a phrase out of the bag and make up a sentence containing that phrase. For some further work, look back at the activities in the unit and experiment with the phrases in each sentence by moving them about, for example: 'The soil was very wet after the rain.' 'After the rain, the soil was very wet.'

Answers
Practice
1-2. *Sentences*
   a) A ghostly sea captain <u>spoke</u> to the girl.
   c) The ship <u>sank</u> in the sea.
   d) The dog <u>chewed</u> the bone.
   g) King Henry <u>was</u> fond of sport.
   h) The sun <u>came</u> out.
   i) <u>Stand</u> up.
   j) The girl <u>ran</u> out of the cave.

Phrases
   b) the silver fish
   e) this morning
   f) yes

Making sure
1. a) The zoo keeper put the vulture back in its cage.
   b) The soil was very wet after the rain.
   c) Three girls climbed over the wall.
   d) Owls come out to hunt at night.
   e) The fire spread through the town.
   f) The football match had to be cancelled because of the fog.
2. (*open*)

Practise your punctuation
1. The lady fried an egg. The hen laid an egg.
2. The man lost his scarf. The cook boiled the potatoes.
3. Fishes swim. Horses trot.
4. The goat ate the grass. The girl sang the song.
5. The builder built the house. The man shaved his chin.
6. The teacher kissed her husband. The doctor roasted her chicken.

Unit 5 Adjectives
Focus
Developing work on adjectives

Definitions of terms used
An adjective is a describing word. Adjectives give us more information about nouns. Adjectives make sentences more interesting.

Teacher's notes
Adjectives can make a piece of work come alive. Demonstrate this by inviting a child to come forward and asking the rest of the class to describe him or her. Ask structured questions like 'What could we say about _____'s hair? eyes?'

Build up a class adjective bank for children to refer to when writing. Divide a large sheet of paper into alphabetical sections, and add interesting adjectives over a period of time.

Look at story books and discuss how boring they would be if all the adjectives were left out.

Answers
Practice
1-8. Several alternative answers are possible for some questions. The important point is that the sentences should make sense. (Use this activity as an opportunity to discuss different possible answers.)

Book 2

Making sure

1. a) The knight fought the dragon.
   b) The wind ripped up the tree.
   c) Some cars sped along the track.
   d) Where have the dinosaurs gone?
   e) The boat was tossed about by the sea.
   f) A man with a hat sang a song.

2. (*open*)

Practise your punctuation

Saturday was a _____ day. Youssef dressed in some _____ clothes. He called for Alice. She lived in a _____ house. They went for a _____ walk in the park. Youssef bought a _____ ice cream. Alice bought a _____ bag of chips. They played on the swings and had a _____ time.

There is an open choice of words to complete the sentences.

Unit 6   Subjects and Verbs

Focus

Introducing the concept of the subject of a sentence

Definitions of terms used

Every sentence has a verb. Every sentence also has a subject. The subject is the main person or thing in the sentence. The subject is usually found in front of the verb.

Teacher's notes

At the simplest level, a sentence can consist of just a subject and a verb: 'Dogs bark.' Brainstorm simple two-word sentences: name an animal and ask the children to supply an appropriate verb, or supply a verb and ask the children to think of a suitable subject to go with it.

After looking at the variety of sentences in the activities in the unit, stress the fact that subjects tend to be nouns (although later children will meet subjects that are pronouns or noun phrases), and tend to precede the verb in a sentence.

Answers

Practice

1. Sandra (saw) a fairy.
2. Dogs (bark).
3. Tortoises (eat) lettuce.
4. The helicopter (crashed).
5. Eddie (followed) the strange troll.
6. Charlie (found) some gold.
7. The snake (slid) through the grass.
8. Sam (won) the race.
9. Curry (is) my favourite dinner.
10. Jack and Jill (went) up the hill.

Making sure

1. a) _____ is a good friend.
   b) _____ swung through the trees.
   c) _____ hunt for food at night.
   d) _____ has lovely handwriting.
   e) _____ buried the treasure.
   f) _____ scared the children.

2. (*open*)

Practise your punctuation

1-2 a) (Penguins) are black and white and live in the Antarctic.
    b) (Little Jack Horner) sat in the corner.
    c) (A shark) has very sharp teeth.
    d) (The space monster) had a pointed head and green teeth.
    e) (Gary Stardust) sang a pop song to the crowd.
    f) (Cows) give us milk, cheese, butter and cream.

Unit 7   Singular and Plural

Focus

Introducing the concept of singular and plural nouns, and the need for subject and verb to agree

Definitions of terms used

We can write nouns in the singular or the plural. **Singular** means 'one'. **Plural** means 'more than one'.

We just add **s** to many singular nouns to make them plural. When a noun ends in a consonant + **y**, we change the **y** to **i** and add **es**.

Teacher's notes

Help children to understand the concept of 'singular' by discussing the word **single**.

The most common way of forming plurals is to add **s**. This unit also deals with nouns ending in a consonant + **y** in the singular. (Further rules for pluralising nouns are covered in Book 3.)

Using reading or information books, see who can collect the most singular and the most plural nouns in five minutes. Use the resulting lists as a basis for discussion. Use the sentences in the unit to reinforce the point that subjects and verbs must always agree.

Answers

Practice

Singular	Plural
school	schools
fly	flies
car	cars
factory	factories
city	cities
picture	pictures
wall	walls
lorry	lorries
spy	spies
lady	ladies

Making sure

1. a) The flies are on the table.
   b) The doors were open.
   c) The stories are boring.
   d) The lorries were speeding.
   e) The dogs are barking loudly.
   f) The factories have lots of windows.

2. a) The picture is very well painted.
   b) The family was sitting on the beach.
   c) The wall was very dirty.
   d) The pony is galloping round the field.
   e) The car is moving on to the ferry.
   f) The city is full of heavy traffic.

Practise your punctuation

1-2 a) The pennies were in the purse.
    b) Some tigers are roaming through the trees.
    c) A horse was eating a carrot.
    d) The baby was drinking a bottle of milk.
    e) Lorries, cars, ships and aeroplanes are all means of transport.
    f) Ponies have manes.

Book 2

Unit 8 Exclamation Marks

Focus
Introducing the concept of exclamation marks

Definitions of terms used
An exclamation mark is a punctuation mark. An exclamation mark comes at the end of a sentence. It shows that the writer feels strongly about something.

It can show excitement or surprise.
It can give warning.
It can show that someone is hurt.
It can show that something happens suddenly.

Teacher's notes
Discuss the fact that people break up their speech into groups of words by pausing, by using a different tone of voice and by accompanying what they say with facial expressions and other non-verbal cues. In writing, we use punctuation marks to break up the text.

An exclamation mark is used when a writer wishes to show strong feeling. Look for examples of exclamation marks in books.

Watch out for a rash of exclamation marks! Children may overuse them at first.

Answers
Practice
Exclamations
Come here quickly!
Help! I'm stuck!
Look what I have found!
I feel quite dizzy!
Smash! Bang! Crash!

Questions
Where are you going?
What is the time?
How do they do that?
Why are you sad?
When can we go home?

Making sure
1-6. (*open*)

Practise your punctuation
1. Is it safe to open the door now?
2. Do not do that!
3. Come here!
4. What do you think you are doing?
5. Hands up! This is a robbery!
6. What is for tea?
7. That is a nasty cut!
8. Help! I am trapped in the mud!

Unit 9 Verb Tenses (past and present)

Focus
Extending the concept of verb tenses (past and present)

Definitions of terms used
Verbs written in the present tense tell us what is happening now. They often have **ing** at the end.

Verbs written in the past tense tell us what happened in the past. They often have **ed** at the end.

Teacher's notes
Introduce this unit by asking children what they did yesterday, at the weekend or during the holidays. Discuss the fact that all these things happened in the past, and that the verbs we use to talk about them are in the past tense.

Ask children to describe the things they are doing now. Explain that the verbs used to describe these things are in the present tense.

Stories tend to be written in the past tense, whereas most information books use the present tense. Collect a few examples of each kind of text.

Answers
Practice
1. Ben <u>is finishing</u> his homework. (present tense)
2. Rosie <u>is helping</u> her mum. (present tense)
3. Joe <u>read</u> a good book yesterday. (past tense)
4. The mouse <u>squeaked</u> loudly. (past tense)
5. On Saturday we <u>walked</u> to the shops. (past tense)
6. The boy <u>smiled</u> at the girl. (past tense)
7. On holiday I <u>visited</u> France. (past tense)
8. The log <u>floated</u> down the river. (past tense)
9. Emma <u>is sitting</u> in the sun. (present tense)
10. The frog <u>hopped</u> on to the rock. (past tense)

Making sure
1. (*open*)
2.
Verb	Present tense	Past tense
wait	Tom is waiting	Tom waited
skip	Tom is skipping	Tom skipped
catch	Tom is catching	Tom caught
eat	Tom is eating	Tom ate

Practise your punctuation
1-2 a) The children <u>are climbing</u> a tree.
   b) Beth <u>is sucking</u> her thumb.
   c) Andy and Dan <u>are playing</u> in the park.
   d) I <u>am writing</u> a poem about a butterfly.
   e) The dog <u>is chasing</u> the postman.
3 a) The children were climbing a tree.
   b) Beth was sucking her thumb.
   c) Andy and Dan were playing in the park.
   d) I was writing a poem about a butterfly.
   e) The dog was chasing the postman.

Unit 10 Adverbs

Focus
Introducing the concept of adverbs (of manner)

Definitions of terms used
An adverb is a word which gives more meaning to a verb. Many adverbs tell us how something happened. Many adverbs of manner ('how' adverbs) end in **ly**.

Teacher's notes
There are three kinds of adverb: adverbs of manner (telling us how an action was performed) such as **brightly**, **quickly**; adverbs of time (telling us when an action was performed) such as **now**, **then**, **always**; and adverbs of place (telling us where an action was performed) such as **here**, **there**. In this unit, only adverbs of manner are dealt with.

To reinforce the unit, play the adverb game. You will need a bag of slips of paper showing adverbs of manner, and a bag of slips of paper showing commands such as 'Hop.' 'Brush your teeth.' Each child has to take a slip from each bag and carry out the command in the manner shown on the adverb slip. This game can be great fun!

Draw particular attention to the various spelling patterns

Book 2

which govern the changing of adjectives into adverbs (page 23). This will prevent many common spelling errors made through lack of understanding.

Answers

Practice

1. a) I eat crisps noisily.
   b) I listen carefully.
   c) I sleep soundly.
   d) I whisper quietly.
   e) I run quickly.
   f) I argue crossly.

2. a) The rain fell <u>heavily</u>.
   b) The river flowed <u>rapidly</u>.
   c) The boy spoke <u>rudely</u>.
   d) Shahla was dressed <u>smartly</u>.
   e) The time passed <u>slowly</u>.
   f) Cross the road <u>safely</u>.
   g) The girl sand <u>loudly</u>.
   h) The nurse treated me <u>gently</u>.

Making sure

1. a) deep – deeply
   b) light – lightly
   c) proud – proudly
   d) clever – cleverly
   e) glad – gladly
   f) fierce – fiercely
   g) clear – clearly
   h) slow – slowly
   i) humble – humbly
   j) noble – nobly
   k) gentle – gently
   l) simple – simply
   m) feeble – feebly
   n) horrible – horribly
   o) sensible – sensibly
   p) terrible – terribly
   q) happy – happily
   r) angry – angrily
   s) heavy – heavily
   t) hungry – hungrily
   u) lucky – luckily
   v) merry – merrily
   w) easy – easily
   x) lazy – lazily

2. (*open*)

Practise your punctuation

1-2. The children were throwing things, running, shouting and laughing. What a noise! Mrs Turner walked <u>quickly</u> down the corridor. She stormed <u>angrily</u> into the room. Mrs Turner shouted <u>loudly</u>. The noise stopped <u>suddenly</u>. The children <u>slowly</u> returned to their seats and got on <u>quietly</u> with their work.

Progress Test A

Answers

1. a) <u>My brother</u> (plays) loud music.
   b) <u>Joanne</u> (sings) very well.
   c) <u>I</u> (am sailing) <u>my boat this morning.</u>.
   d) <u>The passengers</u> (are boarding) the bus.

2. a) Yesterday my brother played loud music.
   b) Yesterday Joanne sang very well.
   c) Yesterday I sailed my boat.
   d) Yesterday the passengers boarded the bus.

3. (*open*)

4.
Common nouns	Proper nouns
bird	Coronation Street
house	Mrs Finch
day	February
holiday	Jupiter
mother	Fernbank Junior School
snow	Holland
envelope	Diwali
	Joanne
	King John

5. (*open*)

6.
Singular	Plural
sock	socks
baby	babies
fly	flies
swimmer	swimmers
shirt	shirts
boat	boats
fly	flies
swimmer	swimmers
story	stories
army	armies
dog	dogs
city	cities

7. a) The puppy in the park was very playful.
   b) The car and the lorry were involved in a serious accident.
   c) The tall trees in the forest made it seem very dark.
   d) Tom was blinded by the bright sunlight.
   e) The stormy weather made the ferry crossing very unpleasant.
   f) It was difficult to move because the streets were so crowded

8. a) Alvin Moonburst <u>is</u> a pop singer who (sings) very well.
   b) The Romans <u>were</u> good soldiers who (fought) bravely.
   c) Dogs (bark) loudly but they <u>are</u> good pets.
   d) The doctor (came) when I <u>was</u> unwell.
   e) I <u>am</u> a good speller and (score) full marks in tests.
   f) Toffees <u>are</u> my favourite sweets and I (eat) lots of them.

Unit 11   Pronouns

Focus
Introducing the concept of pronouns

Definitions of terms used
A pronoun is a word which takes the place of a noun.

Teacher's notes
The prefix **pro** literally means 'in the place of', and **pronoun** means 'in the place of a noun'.

Pronouns help to avoid too much repetition in sentences. They are used very extensively in spoken language when the thing or person being referred to is obvious or visible.

There are various types of pronoun, including personal, possessive, reflexive, relative, demonstrative and interrogative pronouns. This unit deals with some of the personal pronouns. Like nouns, pronouns may be either singular or plural.

Book 2

Answers

Practice
1. The children were sad when they were told off.
2. Rachel said that she was fed up.
3. Do you like chips? Yes, I do!
4. "Pass the ball to me," Tom shouted.
5. Katie asked Harry to give her a sweet.
6. When Dan got home he watched television.
7. Where is the ball? It is under the chair.
8. "Come with us. We are going shopping," the girls said.
9. The birds flew away when the cat chased them.
10. Lisa smiled at Dan. He smiled back at her.

Making sure
1. Pick up your book and put it on the desk.
2. My sister and I are going on holiday because we like the sun.
3. Ben knew exactly what to do when he saw the robber.
4. When the girl walked in the rain she got wet.
5. Mrs Blake gave Tom a hug because she loved him.
6. The race was very important. It turned out to be very exciting.
7. After the woman had read the book she returned it to the library.
8. Ann and I spent the night at a hotel. We left the next morning.

Practise your punctuation
1-2 a) We live in a big house with a large garage. I keep a bike, a sledge, a go-kart and some footballs in it.
  b) Pull the rope hard. If you let it go, the post will fall over.
  c) The television bored me. It was very dull. Even the adverts were boring. They were too old.
  d) We went to the match. Mr Smart gave us a lift.
  e) Joe asked Mrs Crown the way to the shop. She told him how to get there.
  f) Give me an apple please.

Unit 12 Conjunctions

Focus
Introducing the concept of conjunctions

Definitions of terms used
A conjunction (sometimes called a connective) is a joining word. A conjunction is a word we use to join two sentences together to make one longer sentence.

Teacher's notes
The other name for a conjunction (a 'connective') is quite helpful in that it describes what a conjunction does: it connects two sentences to make a longer sentence. (Later in the course, children will be introduced to different types of sentence such as compound and complex sentences.) Some of the most common conjunctions are dealt with in this unit.

When working the activities, point out the fact that one or two words may be changed when two short sentences are joined, to make the new sentence sound better.

Answers

Practice
1. The gorilla looked fierce but it was really rather tame.
2. Jack went to the shop and bought a comic.
3. The referee blew the whistle and the game began.
4. My favourite food is chips but you prefer baked beans.
5. The lion chased the zebra and sprang on to its back.
6. It rained heavily but the game continued.
7. Mum grabbed her umbrella and went out into the rain.
8. Gary did ten spellings but got two wrong.

Making sure
1 a) I went to bed early because I was tired.
  b) I felt sick so we hurried home.
  c) It was raining so we could not go out.
  d) Dan washed his hands because they were dirty.
  e) Jack overslept so he was late for work.
  f) I want something to eat because I am hungry.
  g) The dog barked because a cat was coming.
  h) There was a fire so we shouted for help.

2 a) Mark kept on trying <u>until</u> he passed his driving test.
  b) I hurt my leg <u>when</u> I was playing football.
  c) You must wash up <u>before</u> you go to bed.
  d) I have felt ill <u>since</u> I ate the cake you made.
  e) I washed the car <u>while</u> you were asleep.

Practise your punctuation
1 a) The haunted house was old. It stood in the middle of a dark forest.
  b) The footballer was injured. He was taken to hospital.
  c) The dragon was angry. It was caught in a trap.
  d) The man was lucky. He won the lottery.
  e) The wind was strong. It blew down several trees.
  f) The child was frightened. He ran away to London.

2 a) The old haunted house stood in the middle of a dark forest.
  b) The injured footballer was taken to hospital.
  c) The angry dragon was caught in a trap.
  d) The lucky man won the lottery.
  e) The strong wind blew down several trees.
  f) The frightened child ran away to London.

Unit 13 - More about Adjectives

Focus
Introducing adjectives describing number, order, colour and feeling

Definitions of terms used
An adjective is a describing word. Adjectives tell us more about nouns. Adjectives make writing more interesting.

Teacher's notes
This unit deals with: number adjectives (telling us how many); ordinal adjectives (telling us the order of nouns, such as 'the **first** car'); colour adjectives; and adjectives describing feelings. Stress the fact that all these adjectives describe nouns and give more information, as well as making the text more interesting for the reader.

Answers

Practice
1. (open)

Making sure
1-2. (open)

Practise your punctuation
1-2 a) Have you ever felt <u>lazy</u>? Have you ever wanted to stay in bed all day?
  b) Harry felt <u>happy</u>. He felt <u>contented</u>, <u>satisfied</u>, <u>pleased</u> and <u>delighted</u> all at the same time.

Book 2

c) Edward threw the ball at Sue. Unfortunately, it missed and hit the window. Crash! Mr Clark appeared at the door, looking very <u>angry</u>.

d) It was Shireen's <u>ninth</u> birthday. She had invited <u>four</u> friends to her party. Sam, Nazma, Dan and Dean all came.

Unit 14 Prepositions

Focus
Extending children's understanding of prepositions

Definitions of terms used
A preposition is a word that tells us the position of one thing in relation to another.

Teacher's notes
Look at the word **preposition**. Draw children's attention to the fact that it contains the word **position**. This will help them to remember the function of prepositions.

Demonstrate physically how prepositions work with objects in the classroom, using some of the more common prepositions introduced in the unit.

Answers
Practice
1. The green alien is in the spacecraft.
2. The red alien is on the ladder.
3. The orange alien is climbing into the spacecraft.
4. The blue alien is under the spacecraft.
5. The yellow alien is between the spacecraft and the rock.
6. The purple alien is beside the rock.
7. The pink alien is behind the rock.
8. The brown alien is flying above the rock.

Making sure
There are a number of alternative answers. Here are some possibilities.
1. Tara received a lovely present from her aunt.
2. John draped his coat over a chair.
3. The pirate gold was buried in the ground.
4. Mrs West turned off the light beside her bed.
5. The car raced past the dog at great speed.
6. Jamal ran round the race track twice.
7. The robber threw the stone through the shop window.
8. The car crashed into the traffic lights.
9. The Lottery money was divided between two winners.
10. The magician pulled a rabbit from his hat.

Practise your punctuation
1-2 a) In March the farmer put a fence <u>round</u> his field.
   b) Jenny and Jake sailed their boat <u>down</u> the river.
   c) The jockey fell <u>off</u> his horse.
   d) Our dog Smudge ran <u>across</u> the road.
   e) The swimmer dived <u>into</u> the icy water.
   f) On Sunday, Ben walked his dog <u>through</u> the woods.

Unit 15 Adjectives (comparatives and superlatives)

Focus
Introducing the concept of comparative and superlative adjectives

Definitions of terms used
An adjective is a describing word. When we compare two nouns we use a comparative adjective. When we compare three or more nouns we use a superlative adjective.

Teacher's notes
The comparative and superlative forms of adjectives are used to indicate differences in degree. They both involve comparisons with a baseline: **hot – hotter – hottest**.

Many adjectives take the suffixes **er** (for the comparative) and **est** (for the superlative). The **more/most** (or **less/least**) construction is used when comparing long adjectives.

This unit covers the spelling rules governing the suffixing of adjectives with **er** and **est**.

Answers
Practice

Adjective	Comparative adjective	Superlative adjective
small	smaller	smallest
hard	harder	hardest
new	newer	newest
long	longer	longest
slow	slower	slowest
round	rounder	roundest
fast	faster	fastest
soft	softer	softest
wild	wilder	wildest
sharp	sharper	sharpest

Making sure
1. a) wise – wiser – wisest
   b) brave – braver – bravest
   c) safe – safer – safest
   d) pale – paler – palest
   e) strange – stranger – strangest
   f) tame – tamer – tamest
   g) white – whiter – whitest
   h) large – larger – largest
   i) hot – hotter – hottest
   j) big – bigger – biggest
   k) fat – fatter – fattest
   l) red – redder – reddest
   m) sad – sadder – saddest
   n) wet – wetter – wettest
   o) thin – thinner – thinnest
   p) slim – slimmer – slimmest
   q) busy – busier – busiest
   r) heavy – heavier – heaviest
   s) noisy – noisier – noisiest
   t) lucky – luckier – luckiest
   u) pretty – prettier – prettiest
   v) happy – happier – happiest
   w) ugly – uglier – ugliest
   x) dry – drier – driest

2. a) A rhinoceros is fat. A hippo is fatter but an elephant is fattest.
   b) Ann is pretty. Kim is prettier but Sam is prettiest.
   c) My rabbit is tame. My cat is tamer but my dog is tamest.

Practise your punctuation
1-2 a) Gorillas live in Africa. They are <u>taller</u>, <u>stronger</u>, <u>fiercer</u> and <u>heavier</u> than humans.
   b) The three aliens approached. The red one was hairy and the blue one was <u>hairier</u> still, but the purple one was the (hairiest) thing I have ever seen.

Book 2

Unit 16 Opposites (verbs)

Focus
Opposites (verbs) using prefixes **un** and **dis**

Definitions of terms used
Opposites are words whose meanings are as different as possible from each other. We can sometimes give a verb the opposite meaning by adding a prefix like **un** or **dis** to the beginning of the verb.

Teacher's notes
In Book 1, the concept of opposites was introduced in the context of adjectives. Here, the context is verbs.

The prefixes **un** and **dis** give certain verbs (and certain adjectives) the opposite meaning.

Answers

Practice
1. a) wrap – unwrap
   b) pack – unpack
   c) dress – undress
   d) do – undo
   e) tie – untie
   f) cover – uncover
   g) buckle – unbuckle
   h) bolt – unbolt
2. a) Maria unpacked her case on Saturday.
   b) Ahmed soon got undressed.
   c) The knight unbuckled his belt.
   d) The old lady bolted the door.
   e) Sue wrapped the present carefully.

Making sure
1. a) trust – distrust
   b) agree – disagree
   c) like – dislike
   d) obey – disobey
   e) connect – disconnect
   f) please – displease
   g) appear – disappear
   h) allow – disallow
   i) arm – disarm
2. a) Suddenly, as if by magic, the fluffy white rabbit disappeared.
   b) The football players all disagreed with the referee.
   c) I really dislike sprouts.
   d) The plumber called to disconnect the water supply.
   e) Children always disobey their parents!
   f) Tom knew just how to please his teacher.
   g) The referee allowed the goal.
   h) The bandits were soon armed.
   i) The police officer trusted the shopkeeper.

Practise your punctuation
1. a) Mr Barnes <u>filled</u> the watering can.
   b) Joe, Carra, Mark and Shireen <u>arrived</u> on Friday.
   c) When did you <u>sell</u> that lovely picture?
   d) Mrs Simons <u>lost</u> her purse in the grass.
   e) The children <u>whispered</u> to each other.
   f) The soldiers <u>captured</u> some spies.
2. a) Mr Barnes emptied the watering can.
   b) Joe, Carra, Mark and Shireen left on Friday.
   c) When did you buy that lovely picture?
   d) Mrs Simons found her purse in the grass.
   e) The children shouted to each other.
   f) The soldiers released some spies.

Unit 17 Apostrophes (contractions)

Focus
Introducing apostrophes (in contractions)

Definitions of terms used
An apostrophe is a punctuation mark. We use an apostrophe to show that one or more letters are missing. We sometimes join two words together and miss out some letters. We call these words contractions.
('To contract' means 'to shorten'.)

Teacher's notes
Most punctuation marks are used to mark a pause, to break up groups of words or to indicate the need for a certain tone of voice. The apostrophe, however, does none of these. It may be used: to show a contraction (where a word has been shortened or two words joined together with some letters omitted); or to denote ownership. This unit deals with the first usage.

We tend to use fewer contractions in writing than in speech. Look for examples of contractions in dialogue in stories. Ask children to pronounce the words in full. Discuss how strange it sounds when we speak without using contractions.

Answers

Practice
1. a) couldn't – could not
   b) haven't – have not
   c) aren't – are not
   d) isn't – is not
   e) hasn't – has not
   f) don't – do not
2. a) it is – it's
   b) we are – we're
   c) I have – I've
   d) she would – she'd
   e) we will – we'll
   f) who is – who's
   g) I am – I'm
   h) you have – you've
   i) you are – you're
   j) I would – I'd
   k) we have – we've
   l) he is – he's

Making sure
1. a) I have got a new bike.
   b) I am going to France.
   c) She is a good swimmer.
   d) It is no good. You will have to try harder.
   e) We are having a great time.
   f) I am sure you would like it.
   g) We will all do it together.
   h) It is not fair.
2. a) Don't do it!
   b) I haven't got any money.
   c) The tigers weren't very fierce.
   d) I'll call for you later.
   e) Who's that?
   f) We've scored two goals.
   g) I'd help if I could.
   h) They're in bed.

Practise your punctuation
1-2. Emma: <u>I've</u> got a good joke. Do you want to hear it?
     Edward: I hope <u>it's</u> a good one.

Book 2

Emma: What do you call a camel with three humps?
Edward: I don't know.
Emma: Humphrey!
Edward That's the worst joke you've ever told me!

Unit 18 Sentences (subject and predicate)

Focus
Analysing sentences into subject and predicate

Definitions of terms used
Every simple sentence can be divided into two parts: a subject and a predicate.

The subject is the main thing or person.

The predicate is the rest of the sentence. It always contains a verb which tells us what is happening.

Teacher's notes
This unit revises work on sentence construction, including subjects and verbs. It introduces the idea of dividing sentences into subject and predicate.

Play a game to reinforce this idea. You will need two bags. In one, put several strips of paper showing various subjects, such as 'The fearsome pirate', 'My teacher', 'Children'. In the other bag, put slips showing a variety of predicates, such as 'can swim fast.', 'is beautiful.', 'are noisy.' Ask each child to draw out a subject and predicate. If a sentence makes sense, a point is gained. Be ready for some hilarious sentences!

Answers
Practice
1. The snake slithered through the grass.
2. A grey cat jumped over our fence.
3. Bakers bake bread.
4. Comedians tell jokes.
5. Robin Hood hid in Sherwood Forest.
6. My pet dog was chewing a bone.
7. Some fishing boats chugged out of the harbour.
8. The busy doctor visited the sick child.

Making sure
1-2 a) My youngest brother eats a lot of pizzas.
   b) The big black crow flew into the clear blue sky.
   c) A fierce wild dog snarled at the frightened boy.
   d) Three strong men pushed the car back on to the road.
   e) Some straggly sheep were grazing in the field.
   f) Kieran and Jayesh ran into the cave as fast as they could.
   g) The new dentist inspected my teeth.
   h) The teacher in the playground blew the whistle.
   i) A small fishing boat was battered by the huge waves.
   j) The metal robot moved with strange clanking sounds.

Practise your punctuation
1 a) The hungry tiger pounced on Sara.
  b) The guide dog found the injured explorer on top of the icy mountain.
  c) The police officer chased the young burglar.
  d) A red sports car crashed into the back of the coach.
  e) The dragon ate Prince Rupert for breakfast.
  f) The wise old wizard turned Tess into a toad.
2 a) Sara pounced on the hungry tiger.
  b) The injured explorer found the guide dog on top of the icy mountain.
  c) The young burglar chased the police officer.
  d) The coach crashed into the back of a red sports car.
  e) Prince Rupert ate the dragon for breakfast.
  f) Tess turned the wise old wizard into a toad.

Unit 19 Direct Speech

Focus
Introducing the concept of inverted commas

Definitions of terms used
When we write down the exact words that someone has spoken we call this direct speech. We use inverted commas to mark the beginning and end of what the person said. Everything the person said goes inside the inverted commas.

Teacher's notes
Children will have seen inverted commas (speech marks) in reading books, comics and advertisements. They will probably have included dialogue in their own writing from time to time.

The gradual introduction of the conventions for setting down dialogue is important if the children's writing is to be easy to read. A good way of introducing direct speech is through the use of speech bubbles. This makes it easier to understand that everything the person says goes inside inverted commas.

Children also need to learn that a new line should be started every time a new person speaks; that a capital letter is used for the opening word of a speech (as this is really the beginning of the sentence being spoken); and that the spoken words should be separated from the words which tell the reader who is speaking.

Some printed texts use single inverted commas and some use double. In this unit, double inverted commas are used.

Answers
Practice
1. The lady said, "I would like some soup, please."
2. The waitress asked, "Which soup would you like?"
3. The lady replied, "What sort of soup have you got?"
4. The waitress said, "You can have tomato soup or vegetable soup."
5. The lady said, "I'll have the tomato soup."
6. The waitress replied, "I'll go and get it for you."

Making sure
1-4. (*open*)

Practise your punctuation
1. The troll roared, "Why are you walking on my bridge?"
   Dan replied, "I'm walking because I can't fly!"
2. The car mechanic said, "There's a problem with the steering wheel."
   Mrs Monk asked, "Can you mend it by Saturday?"
3. Mr Ford said, "You can have hamburger, pizza, curry or fish fingers for tea."
   John answered, "I'll have hamburger and chips, please."
4. The teacher asked, "Where do you think you're going?"
   Beth said, "I'm going home for dinner."
5. Jo asked, "What do you call someone who has jelly and custard in their ears?"
   Carra said, "I don't know."
   Jo smiled and said, "A trifle deaf!"

Book 2

Unit 20 Positive and Negative Sentences

Focus

Introducing the concept of positive and negative sentences

Definitions of terms used

A positive word or sentence is one that means 'yes'.
A negative word or sentence is the opposite. It means 'no'.
The main negative in English is **not** or **n't**.

Teacher's notes

Children may have come across the words **positive** and **negative** before, possibly in relation to using batteries where the symbols **+** and **–** are used. Changing a sentence from positive to negative (or *vice versa*) involves altering the verb in some way. (The usual way of expressing a negative is by using **not** or **n't** with the verb.)

Answers

Practice

1.
   a) I am fond of spiders. (positive)
   b) I can't finish this sum. (negative)
   c) I don't like swimming. (negative)
   d) The sun isn't very hot. (negative)
   e) Those animals are very tame. (positive)
   f) Paris is not in Scotland. (negative)
   g) Gary can't ride a bicycle. (negative)
   h) These questions are easy. (positive)
   i) Sasha is the best speller in the class. (positive)
   j) Camping is allowed in the forest. (positive)

2.
   a) I am not fond of spiders.
   b) I can finish this sum.
   c) I like swimming.
   d) The sun is very hot.
   e) Those animals are not very tame.
   f) Paris is in Scotland.
   g) Gary can ride a bicycle.
   h) These questions are not easy.
   i) Sasha is not the best speller in the class.
   j) Camping is not allowed in the forest.

Making sure

1.
   a) The dragon did not blow smoke through its nostrils.
   b) Olivia does not play the guitar.
   c) The fire did not burn for three days.
   d) The giraffe did not eat the leaves from the tree.
   e) Mr Jones did not catch the last bus home.

2.
   a) The washing dried very well.
   b) Henry was a king of England.
   c) Please wear your best clothes.
   d) The hedgehog hibernates in winter.
   e) It's true!

Practise your punctuation

1. Rabbits do not come out to feed early in the morning. They don't sleep during the day in their burrows. Their ears aren't very long so rabbits can't hear very well. They cannot easily escape from their enemies because they are not able to run very fast. Rabbits don't have sharp front teeth. They do not like nibbling carrots and lettuces.

2. Rabbits come out to feed early in the morning. They sleep during the day in their burrows. Their ears are very long so rabbits can hear very well. They can easily escape from their enemies because they are able to run very fast. Rabbits have sharp front teeth. They like nibbling carrots and lettuces.

45

Book 2

Progress Test B

Answers

1. (open)

2.
   a) playing <u>in</u> the park
   b) sitting <u>on</u> a chair
   c) running <u>through</u> the woods
   d) flying <u>over</u> the sea
   e) swimming <u>under</u> the water
   f) standing <u>by</u> a tree
   g) stopping <u>outside</u> a shop
   h) going <u>up</u> the stairs

3.
   a) The boy could not carry the box. It was too heavy for him.
   b) Mrs Bryant bought a new car. She paid a lot for it.
   c) The firefighters fought the fire. They took a long time to put it out.
   d) Hannah keeps goldfish. She feeds them every day.
   e) Sam and Ben have a dog called Sally. They take her for walks.

4.
   a) Dad bought a new suit but it was too big for him.
   b) It was an easy test so I finished it quickly.
   c) I have a drink when I am thirsty.
   d) You will be late for school if you do not hurry.
   e) Sam picked an apple and ate it straight away.
   f) The lady put up her umbrella because it was raining.

5.
   a) (My sister) can stand on her head.
   b) (Our classroom) has thirty desks.
   c) (The sun) shone brightly all day.
   d) (The flag) was very colourful.
   e) (Several horses) galloped around the field.
   f) (The big brown dog) is barking furiously.
   g) (Youssef) wrote a good story.
   h) (The noisy children) were playing football.

6.
   a) My sister cannot stand on her head.
   b) Our classroom does not have thirty desks.
   c) The sun did not shine brightly all day.
   d) The flag was not very colourful.
   e) Several horses did not gallop around the field.
   f) The big brown dog is not barking furiously.
   g) Youssef did not write a good story.
   h) The noisy children were not playing football.

7.

Adjective	Comparative adjective	Superlative adjective
old	older	oldest
long	longer	longest
wet	wetter	wettest
big	bigger	biggest
large	larger	largest
nasty	nastier	nastiest
hard	harder	hardest
white	whiter	whitest

8.
   a) disobey
   b) misunderstand
   c) unscrew
   d) unlock
   e) disapprove
   f) disappear
   g) misbehave
   h) misread
   i) unload
   j) misplace
   k) disown
   l) undo
   m) uncoil
   n) disconnect
   o) miscalculate

9.
   a) A phrase is a small group of words that does not make sense on its own.
   b) Every sentence must contain a verb.
   c) The subject is the main person or thing in the sentence.
   d) We use a plural when we are talking about more than one thing.
   e) The present tense of a verb tells us what is happening now.
   f) An adverb gives more meaning to a verb.
   g) A pronoun takes the place of a noun.
   h) A comparative adjective is used to compare two nouns.

Book 3

Unit	Content
1	Parts of Speech (nouns, adjectives, verbs and adverbs)
2	Types of Sentence
3	Verb Tenses (past)
4	Auxiliary Verbs
5	Adjectives (comparatives and superlatives)
6	Adverbs (of manner, time and place)
7	Using Commas
8	Nouns (singular and plural)
9	Direct Speech
10	Pronouns
	Progress Test A
11	Sentences (subject, verb and object)
12	Possessive Nouns
13	Possessive Adjectives and Possessive Pronouns
14	Phrases
15	Paragraphs
16	Sentences (subject and verb agreement)
17	Prepositions
18	Clauses
19	Indirect Speech
20	Verb Tenses (future)
	Progress Test B

Scope and sequence of skills

Unit	Title	Practice	Making sure	Practise your punctuation
1	**Parts of Speech (nouns, adjectives, verbs and adverbs)** Page 4	Sentence completion using nouns, adjectives, verbs and adverbs	Changing nouns to adjectives, verbs to nouns, and adjectives to adverbs	Capital letters, full stops, question marks, exclamation marks, apostrophes; reinforcing work on adjectives, nouns and verbs
2	**Types of Sentence** Page 6	Writing statements to answer questions	Sequencing commands (instructions); giving contexts for exclamations	Full stops, capital letters, commas, apostrophes, exclamation marks, question marks; reinforcing work on types of sentence
3	**Verb Tenses (past)** Page 8	Forming regular and irregular past tenses; putting sentences into the past tense	Matching present/past tenses; using them in sentences	Capital letters, full stops, inverted commas, commas, exclamation marks, question marks; reinforcing work on verb tenses
4	**Auxiliary Verbs** Page 10	Sentence completion using given auxiliary verbs	Identifying and using auxiliary verbs	Capital letters, full stops, commas, question marks, inverted commas; reinforcing work on auxiliary verbs
5	**Adjectives (comparatives and superlatives)** Page 12	Writing the comparative and superlative forms of given adjectives	Writing the comparative and superlative forms of given adjectives	Capital letters, full stops; reinforcing work on comparative and superlative adjectives
6	**Adverbs (of manner, time and place)** Page 14	Identifying verbs and adverbs of manner; using adverbs of time and place in sentences	Classifying adverbs	Capital letters, full stops, commas, apostrophes; reinforcing work on adverbs

47

Book 3

Unit	Title	Practice	Making sure	Practise your punctuation
7	**Using Commas** Page 16	Punctuating lists with commas; punctuating sentences with commas	Punctuating sentences with commas	Capital letters, commas, full stops; punctuating sentences
8	**Nouns (singular and plural)** Page 18	Forming and matching singular and plural nouns (regular and irregular)	Completing phrases with plural nouns and collective nouns	Capital letters, full stops, commas, inverted commas, question marks, exclamation marks; reinforcing work on singular and plural nouns and subject/verb agreement
9	**Direct Speech** Page 20	Punctuating given sentences with inverted commas	Punctuating given sentences with inverted commas	Rewriting a playscript as a conversation using inverted commas and other punctuation
10	**Pronouns** Page 22	Sentence completion using given pronouns	Sentence completion using **I** or **me**	Capital letters, full stops, commas, question marks, exclamation marks, inverted commas; reinforcing work on pronouns
	Progress Test A Page 24	Revising and testing aspects of grammar taught in previous ten units		
11	**Sentences (subject, verb and object)** Page 26	Choosing suitable objects to complete sentences; dividing sentences into subject, verb and object	Expanding sentences, changing pronouns into nouns; dividing sentences into subject, verb and object	Using punctuation; composing sentences using given words; reinforcing work on subject, verb and object
12	**Possessive Nouns** Page 28	Writing sentences containing possessive nouns (singular)	Writing sentences containing possessive nouns (singular and plural)	Capital letters, full stops, commas, exclamation marks, apostrophes; reinforcing work on possessive nouns
13	**Possessive Adjectives and Possessive Pronouns** Page 30	Identifying possessive adjectives in sentences; replacing possessive nouns with possessive adjectives	Completing given sentences with possessive pronouns	Capital letters, full stops, inverted commas, question marks, apostrophes; reinforcing work on possessive adjectives and possessive pronouns
14	**Phrases** Page 32	Completing given sentences with noun and verb phrases	Supplying suitable noun and verb phrases to complete sentences	Capital letters, full stops, commas, inverted commas, exclamation marks; reinforcing work on phrases
15	**Paragraphs** Page 34	Suggesting suitable headings for given paragraphs; writing paragraphs on given subjects	Writing a three-paragraph story based on given pictures; writing two paragraphs supporting opposite arguments; continuing a story, given the first paragraph	Punctuating a passage accurately and dividing it into three paragraphs
16	**Sentences (subject and verb agreement)** Page 36	Selecting correct form of verb to complete given sentences; identifying subject and verb in given sentences; selecting singular and plural nouns to go with given verbs	Conjugating the verbs **to be**, **to do** and **to have**; choosing correct forms of verbs to complete given sentences	Capital letters, full stops, question marks, commas, apostrophes; reinforcing work on subject/verb agreement and singular and plural

Book 3

Unit	Title	Practice	Making sure	Practise your punctuation
17	**Prepositions** Page 38	Matching pairs of prepositions with opposite meanings; completing sentences with suitable prepositions	Completing given sentences with suitable prepositions	Capital letters, full stops, question marks, commas; reinforcing work on prepositions
18	**Clauses** Page 40	Supplying suitable subjects and predicates to complete sentences; dividing given sentences into subject and predicate; identifying verbs	Joining two one-clause sentences together with a conjunction to make a two-clause sentence	Capital letters, full stops, commas; reinforcing work on clauses
19	**Indirect Speech** Page 42	Changing direct speech into indirect speech	Changing indirect speech into direct speech	Capital letters, full stops, apostrophes, question marks, commas, exclamation marks; converting a playscript into indirect speech
20	**Verb Tenses (future)** Page 44	Changing present tense to future tense and *vice versa*	Writing verbs in present, past and future tenses; changing verbs in passage from past to future tense	Capital letters, full stops, commas, apostrophes, exclamation marks; reinforcing work on verb tenses
	Progress Test B Page 46	Revising and testing aspects of grammar taught in previous ten units		

Book 3

Unit 1 Parts of Speech (nouns, adjectives, verbs and adverbs)

Focus
Developing the concept of parts of speech, with reference to nouns, adjectives, verbs and adverbs

Definitions of terms used
Grammar is the study of the way in which we use words to make sentences. Words may be divided into groups called 'parts of speech'. Four important parts of speech are: nouns, adjectives, verbs and adverbs.

Teacher's notes
Words may be divided into groups according to their function (the way in which they are used in sentences). Parts of speech are sometimes called 'word classes'.

There are eight main parts of speech in English: nouns, adjectives, verbs, adverbs, prepositions, conjunctions, pronouns and articles. The term 'parts of speech' is slightly deceptive because these word groups are found in writing as well as in speech.

Answers
Practice
1. a) I could see the silver fish in the water.
   b) The fat frog hopped into the pond.
   c) The small bird flapped its wings because it was frightened.
2. a) The driver hooted his horn and shook his fist angrily.
   b) Megan ate her sandwiches quickly and drank her drink thirstily.
   c) The waiter put the tray down gently when he served our drinks.

Making sure

1.

Noun	Adjective
anger	angry
beauty	beautiful
comfort	comfortable
danger	dangerous
expense	expensive
fame	famous
nation	national
history	historic
wool	woollen
fury	furious

2.

Verb	Noun
act	action
arrive	arrival
behave	behaviour
compare	comparison
deliver	delivery
encourage	encouragement
enter	entrance
hate	hatred
marry	marriage
press	pressure

3.

Adjective	Adverb
clever	cleverly
clear	clearly
wide	widely
rough	roughly
able	ably
bad	badly
careful	carefully
lucky	luckily
noisy	noisily
faithful	faithfully

Practise your punctuation

1-2 a) Have you seen my <u>ring</u>(n)? I've lost it. <u>Ring</u>(v) me up if you find it.
   b) Tom took the <u>sweet</u>(a) apple but Vicky took the <u>sweet</u>(n).
   c) Crash! The <u>lift</u>(n) broke when I tried to <u>lift</u>(v) the heavy case into it.
   d) The archaeologist found a large <u>stone</u>(n) inside the <u>stone</u>(a) vase.

Unit 2 Types of Sentence

Focus
Introducing the four different types of sentence

Definitions of terms used
There are four different types of sentence:
- statements
- questions
- commands
- exclamations.

A statement is a sentence which gives us information.

A question asks something. A question finishes with a question mark.

A command tells someone to do something.

An exclamation shows that a person feels something strongly. An exclamation finishes with an exclamation mark.

Teacher's notes
The statement is the most common type of sentence.

Many questions begin with question words (such as **what**), or have a different word order from statements, or both.

A command usually takes the simple form of the verb, as in 'Take some sweets.' There is usually no subject in a command as the subject **you** is understood.

We use exclamations when we want to express something with feeling.

In writing, questions, commands and exclamations usually have different patterns from statements, but in speech this is not necessarily always the case, as it often depends on the way in which something is said.

Answers
Practice
1. (open)
2. a) Does Jo often copy Kimberley's work?
   b) Is Khayyam's book very messy?
   c) Did Mrs Saunders shout at Bethany?
   d) Was the dragon long and thin?
   e) Is Andrea good at art?
   f) Are there such things as unicorns?

Making sure
1. <u>Get</u> a lump of moist clay.
   <u>Roll</u> the clay into a round ball.
   <u>Make</u> a pot shape.
   <u>Smooth</u> the outside of your pot.
   <u>Leave</u> your pot to dry.
   <u>Put</u> your dry pot into a kiln.
   <u>Heat</u> the kiln to bake your pot.
2. (open)

Practise your punctuation

1-2 a) How far is it to the Houses of Parliament? q
   b) Bring me my book, pencil, ruler and crayons, Jack. c

c) We're all going to Jamaica for our summer holiday. s
d) My house is on fire! e

Unit 3   Verb Tenses (past)

Focus
Extending children's understanding of the past tense and how to form it

Definitions of terms used
Verbs written in the past tense tell us what happened some time ago.

Some verbs add **d** or **ed** to make the past tense.

Some verbs change the middle vowel sound to make the past tense.

Some verbs change completely to make the past tense.

Teacher's notes
The tense of a verb tells us when something happened. Verbs written in the past tense tell of events that happened in the past.

English is a fascinating language because of its varied etymology. This does mean that it is not always entirely straightforward or predictable. It is interesting to note how toddlers begin to apply 'rules' when learning to speak, for example, 'He **comed**' instead of 'He **came**'. There are many verbs which do not simply take **ed** in the past tense. This unit deals with some of them.

Answers
Practice
1. a) get – got
   b) sit – sat
   c) give – gave
   d) sing – sang
   e) fall – fell
   f) throw – threw
   g) hold – held
   h) dig – dug
   i) stick – stuck
   j) sink – sank
   k) begin – began
   l) ride – rode
   m) grow – grew
   n) blow – blew
   o) swim – swam
2. a) I held the baby gently in my arms.
   b) I dug the garden with a fork.
   c) I got hot in the sun.
   d) I sang in the bath.
   e) I sat in the most comfortable chair.
   f) I rode my bike in the park.
   g) I swam in the sea.
   h) I began my meal with a bowl of soup.

Making sure
1. is – was, are – were, think – thought, buy – bought, say – said, keep – kept, feel – felt, sleep – slept, leave – left, go – went, do – did, kneel – knelt, catch – caught, have – had, wear – wore, eat – ate
2. a) Last week my mum bought me a new school uniform.
   b) The teacher said , "I thought that was very silly!"
   c) We were working very hard.
   d) When I slept in the tent, I kept a torch under my pillow.
   e) Yesterday I left my bag at school by mistake.
   f) A short while ago I caught a very bad cold.
   g) I went up to my bedroom for a bit of peace.

Practise your punctuation
1-2 a) Harry <u>sits</u> on the settee and <u>turns</u> on the television. pr
   b) The teacher <u>asked</u>, "Who <u>threw</u> that book?" pa
   c) The train to Luton <u>stops</u> at every station. pr
   d) I <u>creep</u> up the stairs quietly and <u>frighten</u> my brother. pr
   e) Beth and Alice <u>rode</u> their bikes home on Saturday. pa
   f) <u>Stop</u>! <u>Come</u> here at once! pr
   g) Yesterday we <u>saw</u> lots of interesting things on our trip. pa
   h) At the shop Amy <u>bought</u> some apples, pears, bananas and grapes. pa

Unit 4   Auxiliary Verbs

Focus
Introducing the concept of auxiliary verbs

Definitions of terms used
Sometimes we need an extra verb to help the main verb to work properly. These 'helper' verbs are called auxiliary verbs.

Teacher's notes
Two or more words are used to make up certain forms of a verb: '**I am hopping**,' '**I will be hopping**.' Verbs such as **am** or **will** are called auxiliary verbs.

Look through a passage with the class to see how many different auxiliary verbs can be found.

Answers
Practice
1. Jane has put a collar and lead on her dog.
2. Amtiaz is going to the pet shop today.
3. Bert can make his parrot talk.
4. Do you know much food a dinosaur ate every day?
5. I have just visited the vet with my pet rabbit.
6. Last week Ann did not go out because she was not feeling well.
7. Yesterday the kittens were rolling on the ground. Today they are sleeping quietly.

Making sure
1. These auxiliary verbs are hidden in the puzzle: **must, does, may, am, will, might, could, did, can, would**
2. a) Next week I am having a party.
   b) "Will you marry me?" the prince asked the princess.
   c) Last week Mum thought she might win the Lottery.
   d) You must leave quickly when the fire alarm sounds.
   e) If you could become anyone you wished, who would you choose to be?
   f) "Did you really try hard with your writing?" the teacher asked.
   g) Jenny can say the alphabet backwards.
   h) "You may go out to play if you like," said Mrs Bakhtiar.
   i) How long does it take to reach the shops?

Practise your punctuation
1 a) Ann <u>is</u> training to be a vet.
   b) The lady <u>was</u> buying potatoes, cabbages, carrots and onions.

Book 3

c) I <u>should</u> have scored the winning goal but I missed.
d) One day a spaceship <u>will</u> land on Mars.
e) If I try hard I <u>may</u> get better at spelling.
f) "<u>Would</u> you like a new pair of trainers?" asked Mrs Smith.
g) Mrs James saw Sharon and said, "I <u>do</u> like your new top."

2. is, was, should, will, may, would, do

Unit 5   Adjectives (comparatives and superlatives)

Focus
Extending children's understanding of comparative and superlative adjectives

Definitions of terms used
An adjective is a describing word.

When we compare two nouns, we use a comparative adjective. When we compare three or more nouns, we use a superlative adjective.

When the adjective is short, the comparative form usually ends in **er**. When the adjective is short, the superlative form usually ends in **est**.

When an adjective is long, it sounds strange to add **er** or **est**. We use the word **more** to make the comparative form. We use the word **most** to make the superlative form.

Teacher's notes
The comparative and superlative forms of an adjective are used to indicate differences in degree. They both involve comparisons with a baseline: **hot – hotter – hottest**.

Answers
Practice

	Adjective	Comparative adjective	Superlative adjective
1.	wise	wiser	wisest
2.	big	bigger	biggest
3.	happy	happier	happiest
4.	beautiful	more beautiful	most beautiful
5.	comfortable	more comfortable	most comfortable
6.	dangerous	more dangerous	most dangerous

Making sure
1. bright – brighter – brightest
2. bad – worse – worst
3. delightful – more delightful – most delightful
4. funny – funnier – funniest
5. terrible – more terrible – most terrible
6. good – better – best
7. pretty – prettier – prettiest
10. many – more – most
11. honest – more honest – most honest
12. wet – wetter – wettest
13. foolish – more foolish – most foolish
14. natural – more natural – most natural
15. musical – more musical – most musical

Practise your punctuation
1-2 a) Mrs Turner is rich <u>but</u> Mr Barnes is <u>richer</u>. Mrs Bates is the <u>richest</u>.
b) Sheep are noisy <u>but</u> cows are <u>noisier</u>. Cockerels are by far the <u>noisiest</u> of the farm animals.
c) One slice of pizza is good. <u>Two</u> slices of pizza are <u>better</u>. The whole pizza is <u>best</u>.
d) The Smith family is very quarrelsome but the Brown family is even <u>more quarrelsome</u>. The Parker family is the <u>most quarrelsome</u> family in our street.
e) Two meals a day is <u>bad</u>. One meal a day is <u>worse</u>. No meals a day is <u>worst</u> of all.

Unit 6   Adverbs (of manner, time and place)

Focus
Extending children's understanding of the three types of adverb

Definitions of terms used
An adverb is a word which gives more meaning to a verb.
An adverb of manner tells us how something happened.
An adverb of time tells us when something happened.
An adverb of place tells us where something happened.

Teacher's notes
There are three main types of adverb: adverbs of manner (**brightly**, **quickly**); adverbs of time (**now**, **then**, **always**); adverbs of place (**here**, **there**).

Answers
Practice
1-2 a) The snow <u>fell</u> <u>thickly</u>.
b) <u>Listen</u> <u>carefully</u>.
c) It <u>rained</u> <u>heavily</u> on the tent.
d) I <u>hit</u> the table <u>angrily</u> with my fist.
e) Sara <u>wrote</u> the letter <u>neatly</u>.
f) A tear <u>slowly</u> <u>trickled</u> down my cheek.
g) The cat <u>stretched</u> <u>lazily</u>.
h) The dog <u>ate</u> his dinner <u>greedily</u>.
i) Tom <u>threw</u> the ball <u>accurately</u>.
j) <u>Slowly</u> the giant <u>stretched</u> his arms and legs.

3. (*open*)

Making sure
Adverbs of manner
quickly
gently
suspiciously
tidily
bravely
sweetly
deeply
carefully

Adverbs of time
later
often
yesterday
afterwards
now
next
then
finally
always

Adverbs of place
in
out
inside
everywhere
here
there
up

Practise your punctuation

1-2. Yesterday , I saw two birds busily building their nest.
     (t above Yesterday, m above busily)
They flew backwards and forwards, up and down,
     (p above each underlined word)
and in and out. First, they found some twigs. Next,
     (p, p, t, t above underlined words)
they carefully wove them into a nest. They
     (m above carefully)
tirelessly pulled and tugged it into shape.
     (m above tirelessly)
This wasn't all they did. Finally, they carefully lined
     (t above Finally, m above carefully)
it with moss. Soon, the female bird will lay her eggs.
     (t above Soon)

8. Should I put vinegar on the chips, or not? Yes, you should.
9. Hello, Mr Salim. It's very hot, isn't it?
10. In a cave on the far side of the mountain, there lived a dragon.
11. Louise, who was only nine, easily won the race.
12. St George, brave and valiant, saved the maiden.

Practise your punctuation

1. The king walked and talked. Half an hour after, his head was cut off.
2. The soldier entered, on his head, a helmet, on each foot, a sandal. In his hand, he had his trusty sword.
3. The giant had hairy feet, huge and flat. On his head, he squashed his hat. Over his shoulder, he carried a club, big and spiky. In his hand, a sword he waved.

Unit 7   Using Commas

Focus
Extending the use of commas

Definitions of terms used
A comma is a punctuation mark. Commas show us where to take a slight pause. Commas help us to understand the meaning of a sentence.

Teacher's notes
Discuss the fact that people break up their speech into groups of words by pausing, by using a different tone of voice, and by accompanying what they say with facial expressions and other non-verbal cues. In writing, we use punctuation marks to break up the text.

The use of the comma in lists was introduced earlier in the course. This unit deals with other occasions where a slight pause is needed to separate elements of a sentence and so aid understanding.

The use of commas between direct speech and the group of words telling the reader who spoke is dealt with in Unit 9.

Answers
Practice

1. a) a nasty, mean, spiteful man
   b) dirty, careless, scruffy writing
   c) hot, bright, sunny days
   d) some cold, clear, sparkling water
   e) a huge, angry, lumbering monster
   f) a cool, shady, leafy forest
2. a) The Pyramids, which are in Egypt, are enormous.
   b) Barney, who came last, was very upset.
   c) Mr Younnas, our next-door neighbour, is very nice.
   d) However hard she tried, Wendy could not catch any fish.
   e) We arrived in Paris, the capital of France.
   f) Jane, my sister, is good at singing.
   g) The River Thames, a very long river, flows through London.
   h) Visit Australia, the land of opportunity.

Making sure

1. Dogs don't wear glasses, do they?
2. What's the matter, Johnny?
3. Oh, dear, the lift is stuck!
4. Half an hour later, Sophie came out of the cinema.
5. Please, sir, can you help me?
6. From Monday to Friday, the shop closes at five o'clock.
7. If you turn left, you will soon come to the park.

Unit 8   Nouns (singular and plural)

Focus
Extending children's understanding of singular and plural nouns; introducing collective nouns

Definitions of terms used
We can write nouns in the singular or the plural. **Singular** means 'just one'. **Plural** means 'more than one'.

Most nouns just take **s** to change the singular into the plural form.

Many nouns ending in **f** or **fe** take **ves** in the plural.

Many nouns ending in **o** take **es** in the plural.

Nouns which are the names of groups of people or things are called collective nouns.

Teacher's notes
Further rules for pluralising nouns are introduced in this unit.

Note that a few nouns ending in **f** do not follow the rule. Similarly, although most nouns ending in **o** take **es** in the plural, there are some exceptions.

Using reading or information books, see who can collect the most singular and the most plural nouns in five minutes. Use the resulting lists as a basis for discussion. Use the work in the unit to reinforce the point that subjects and verbs must always agree.

Answers
Practice

1. a) thief – thieves
   b) dog – dogs
   c) hero – heroes
   d) neighbour – neighbours
   e) leaf – leaves
   f) wife – wives
   g) echo – echoes
   h) wolf – wolves
   i) letter – letters
   j) tomato – tomatoes
2. a) volcano
   b) half
   c) life
   e) dingo
   f) loaf
   g) step
   h) cargo
   i) domino
   j) calf

Book 3

3. woman – women, goose – geese, foot – feet, deer – deer, child – children, tooth – teeth

Making sure

1. Some possible answers are:
   a) a pack of cards, wolves
   b) a herd of cattle, cows
   c) a team of horses, footballers
   d) a shoal of fish
   e) a library of books
   f) a swarm of bees, wasps, locusts
   g) a forest of trees
   h) a pile of rubbish, bricks
2. Some possible answers are:
   a) a bunch, hand of bananas
   b) a flotilla, fleet of ships
   c) a gang of thieves
   d) a pack, deck of cards
   e) a group, choir of singers
   f) a litter of kittens
   g) a sheaf of arrows
   h) a suit of clothes

Practise your punctuation

1-2 a) This morning the <u>thieves</u> were arrested.
   b) The baker said, "Sam, put the <u>loaves</u> on the <u>shelves</u>, please."
   c) Are the baked <u>potatoes</u> ready yet?
   d) During the night the <u>leaves</u> fell off the <u>trees</u>.
   e) Mr Smith, the <u>tomatoes</u> you sold me were rotten!

3 a) This morning the thief was arrested.
   b) The baker said, "Sam, put the loaf on the shelf, please."
   c) Is the baked potato ready yet?
   d) During the night the leaf fell off the tree.
   e) Mr Smith, the tomato you sold me was rotten!

Unit 9 Direct Speech

Focus

Developing the use of inverted commas in direct speech

Definitions of terms used

When we write down the exact words someone has spoken, we call this direct speech. We use inverted commas to mark the beginning and end of what the person says.

Teacher's notes

The gradual introduction of the conventions for setting down dialogue is important if children's writing is to be made easy to read.

Children need to be reminded that everything the person says goes inside the inverted commas or speech marks. See the notes on Unit 19 of Book 2 for more suggestions.

Answers

Practice

1. "Wait here," the teacher said.
2. The boy shouted, "Catch the ball."
3. "Please let me go," begged the thief.
4. The old lady said, "Don't worry. I won't hurt you."
5. "I'm going to get an ice cream," the small girl squealed excitedly.
6. "Cut down that tree," commanded the woodcutter.
7. "I'm lost. Which way is it to Ipswich?" enquired the motorist.
8. James asked, "What time is it?"
9. "The house is on fire! Get out of here fast!" shouted Jenna.
10. "I'm hungry. It must be nearly home time," whispered Anna.

Making sure

1. "Help!" screamed Emma. "I'm drowning!"
2. "Sit down," said the teacher, "and get on with your work."
3. "Can I be of assistance?" the shopkeeper asked. "Is there anything I can show you?"
4. "Look at this picture!" exclaimed Francis. "It's really lovely!"
5. "Quick! Pass the ball," shouted Lee. "No one is marking me!"
6. "I can't come out," explained Indira. "I've got too much homework."
7. "I dropped my ring somewhere," explained Ann, "but I can't seem to find it."
8. "I'll meet you in town," Mrs Turner said, "outside the supermarket."
9. "You're early," said the waiter. "Your table is not ready yet."
10. "It's no use crying," snapped Nina's mum. "You will only make things worse."

Practise your punctuation

1-4. There are several different ways of setting the conversation out. Try to encourage a variety of ways of expressing the word **said**.

Unit 10 Pronouns

Focus

Extending children's understanding of pronouns

Definitions of terms used

A pronoun is a word which takes the place of a noun.

Teacher's notes

The prefix **pro** literally means 'in the place of', and **pronoun** means 'in the place of a noun'.

Pronouns help us to avoid too much repetition. They are used extensively in spoken language when the thing or person being referred to is obvious or visible

There are various types of pronoun, including personal, possessive, relative, demonstrative and interrogative pronouns. This unit deals with some personal pronouns in sentences, as subjects (**I**), as objects (**me**) and in the reflexive form (**myself**). Like nouns, pronouns may be singular or plural.

The pronouns **I** and **me** are often confused. If the word is part of the subject of a sentence, use **I**. If it is part of the predicate of a sentence, use **me**. In a list, **I** or **me** always comes at the end.

Answers

Practice

1. I like these sweets. They are my favourites.
2. Ben put his book down. In the morning he could not find it anywhere.
3. When Gemma was undressed she got into the bath.
4. Mrs Smith ran after Sam and me. She chased us down the path.
5. The girl listened to her father because she thought he was right.
6. Don't climb the cliffs or you might hurt yourself.
7. When the dog got wet it shook itself all over Jake!

8. Peter washed himself until he was completely clean.
9. The man gave a present to his wife. He wrapped it before he gave it to her.
10. We got top marks in the test. We were very pleased with ourselves.

Making sure
1. Will and I are eating fish and chips.
2. The teacher gave the book to James and me.
3. The dog belongs to Jason and me.
4. My dad and I went to the cinema last night.
5. My cat and I both like milk.
6. Tom does not like Shannon and me.
7. Gran spilled her drink over George and me.
8. My friend and I went shopping.
9. Francis invited Richard and me to tea.
10. Uncle Bob and I enjoy playing football.

Practise your punctuation
1-2 a) 'Get up, Mark, or <u>you</u> will be late for school!' shouted Mr Bentall.
   b) The bike has a puncture. Where can <u>I</u> get <u>it</u> mended?
   c) Emma likes crisps, biscuits, sweets and ice creams. <u>They</u> are all bad for <u>her</u>.
   d) Last night Dean and <u>I</u> went to see a film. <u>We</u> liked <u>it</u> very much.
   e) 'Shall <u>we</u> catch the bus or the train?' Mrs Croft asked <u>us</u>.
   f) Help! An alien has landed! <u>It</u> is coming to get <u>me</u>!

Progress Test A

Answers

1 a) The brown dog barked loudly. (adj n v adv)
  b) Suddenly an enormous snake appeared. (adv adj n v)
  c) The noisy girls chatted excitedly. (adj n v adv)
  d) Quietly the burglar crept along the stone path. (adv n v adj n)

2 a) How are you? q
  b) Come here. c
  c) I am going to school. s
  d) I feel terrible! e

3 a) catch – caught
  b) hug – hugged
  c) run – ran
  d) live – lived
  e) hold – held
  f) tell – told
  g) swim – swam
  h) write – wrote
  i) walk – walked
  j) cut – cut

4.
Adjective	Comparative adjective	Superlative adjective
bright	brighter	brightest
pretty	prettier	prettiest
helpful	more helpful	most helpful
anxious	more anxious	most anxious
heavy	heavier	heaviest
bad	worse	worst
good	better	best

5 a) The frog <u>can</u> jump very high.
  b) She <u>must</u> go to the shops.
  c) Ben <u>has</u> scored a goal.
  d) The spacecraft <u>will</u> reach Venus.

6.
Adverbs of manner	Adverbs of time	Adverbs of place
softly	after	there
loudly	next	down
wearily	now	here
quickly	lastly	inside

7 a) echo – echoes
  b) thief – thieves
  c) woman – women
  d) child – children
  e) potato – potatoes
  f) wife – wives

8 a) a flock of sheep, birds
  b) a bunch of grapes
  c) an army of soldiers, ants
  d) a shoal of fish
  e) a choir of singers, angels
  f) a herd of cows

9 a) I like baked beans. They are delicious.
  b) Ellen took her trainers off. She forgot to put them in her bag.
  c) When Edward got home he did his homework.
  d) Mr Bryant's dog was enormous but it was quite tame.

10 a) Lauren and I are going to school.
   b) Mrs McDonald gave Matthew and me a drink.
   c) My friend and I went to the park.
   d) Our neighbour likes my dog and me.

Unit 11 Sentences (subject, verb and object)

Focus
Revising work on sentence analysis, involving subjects and verbs; introducing the concept of the object

Definitions of terms used
Every sentence must have a subject and a verb.

Some sentences also have an object. The object is the person or thing that is affected by the verb. The object usually comes after the verb in a sentence. Not all verbs can have an object.

Teacher's notes
Introduce the unit by revising the concept of the subject (the main person, place or thing in the sentence) and the concept of the verb, and the fact that every sentence must have a subject and a verb.

The unit then deals with transitive verbs (verbs that take an object). At this stage, children do not need to know the term 'transitive', but they do need to understand what an object is.

Children may know that in snooker, the ball being aimed at is called the object ball. It is the ball which is being affected. The object in a sentence is the word being affected by the verb.

Some verbs may be transitive or intransitive: 'I am **playing** tennis.' 'I am **playing**.'

Answers
Practice
1-2. (*open*)

Book 3

Making sure
1-2. (*open*)

Practise your punctuation
1-2. (*open*)

Unit 12   Possessive Nouns

Focus
Introducing the use of the apostrophe to indicate ownership in possessive nouns

Definitions of terms used
A possessive noun tells us who the owner of something is. We use an apostrophe to help make a possessive noun.

If there is just one owner, we add **'s** to make the noun a possessive noun. ('my **mother's** cottage')

When there is more than one owner, we add **'** to the plural noun ending in **s** to make it a possessive noun.
('the **teachers'** car park')

When the plural does not end in **s**, we add **'s**.
('the **children's** books')

Teacher's notes
Apostrophes denoting ownership are difficult to grasp. The three simple rules in the definitions above are basically all the children need to know.

There is always a danger that if these rules are not grasped, children's work will suddenly 'sprout' apostrophes all over the place. Discourage inappropriate use of them.

We only write **it's** and **who's** when forming the contractions of **it is** and **who is**.

Answers
Practice
1. It is the burglar's torch.
2. It is the woman's glove.
3. It is the robber's car.
4. They are the teacher's pencils.
5. It is Mr Patel's shop.
6. It is Lisa's bike
7. It is the gorilla's banana.
8. It is Fido's lead.
9. They are Mark's trousers.
10. It is the queen's ring.

Making sure
1. a) The cave belongs to the dragons.
   b) The cars belong to the men.
   c) The skirts belong to the ladies.
   d) The saddles belong to the horses.
   e) The bedroom belongs to the girls.
   f) The doors belong to the churches.
2. In each case, the first possessive noun is singular and the second is plural.

Practise your punctuation
1. Doctor Turner's car was dirty, rusty and badly repaired.
2. Mrs Banks, who was getting very angry, shouted, "Pass me Sam's trousers, will you?"
3. His sister's name was Alice.
4. Harry's house was near Mr Clarke's field.
5. "Don't pull the crocodile's tail or it'll bite you!" warned the zoo keeper.
6. The babies' clothes were hanging on the line.

Unit 13   Possessive Adjectives and Possessive Pronouns

Focus
Introducing possessive adjectives and possessive pronouns

Definitions of terms used
A possessive adjective tells us who the owner of something is.

A possessive pronoun tells us the same thing.

Possessive adjectives and possessive pronouns do not take an apostrophe.

Teacher's notes
The possessive adjectives are: **my**, **your**, **his**, **her**, **its**, **our**, **their**. They are also pronouns, but it is easier to think of them as adjectives as they precede, and describe, nouns.

The possessive pronouns are: **mine**, **yours**, **his**, **hers**, **ours**, **theirs**.

Discourage the inappropriate use of apostrophes.

Answers
Practice
1. a) <u>Our</u> school is the best.
   b) "Where is <u>your</u> friend?" <u>my</u> dad called.
   c) Sara wore <u>her</u> new dress and William wore <u>his</u> new trainers.
   d) The lost dog found <u>its</u> way home.
   e) Indira and Karen looked for <u>their</u> shoes.
2. a) Ben bought his comic at the shop.
   b) Emma spent all her money on sweets.
   c) Alan and Alice went off on their bikes.
   d) Our car is in the garage.
   e) This is my telescope.

Making sure
1. This cat belongs to me. It is mine.
2. That cat belongs to you. It is yours.
3. The green car belongs to him. It is his.
4. You must take the responsibility.
   The responsibility is yours.
5. The red van belongs to them. It is theirs.
6. The books on the table belong to Tim and me.
   They are ours.
7. Sally has taken the books that belong to her.
   They are hers.
8. I think the blue pencils belong to you.
   They must be yours.
9. I found the money so it is mine now.
10. Do these slippers belong to you? Are they yours?

Practise your punctuation

1-2. On <u>his</u>^{pa} way home from school, Tom found a bag on the ground. "Is this <u>yours</u>^{pp}?" he asked Tara.

"No, it's not <u>my</u>^{pa} bag. I left <u>mine</u>^{pp} at school. I think it might be Emma's bag because <u>hers</u>^{pp} is blue and green."

Tom laughed and said, "You may be right. She is always losing <u>her</u>^{pa} things."

The two children picked up the bag and continued on <u>their</u>^{pa} way.

Book 3

Unit 14 Phrases

Focus
Extending children's understanding of phrases

Definitions of terms used
A phrase is a group of words which forms part of a sentence. Phrases are usually quite short. They do not make sense on their own.

Teacher's notes
This unit develops work covered in Book 2. A phrase is a group of words which does not make sense on its own. It may be helpful for children to see phrases as part of the hierarchy 'word - phrase - sentence'.

Phrases can be divided into five groups:
Noun phrases: 'a slimy **mud** puddle'
Verb phrases: '**staggered** about'
Adjective phrases: 'more and more **beautiful**'
Adverb phrases: 'as **slowly** as possible'
Preposition phrases: '**on** the kitchen table'
This unit deals with the first two.

Answers
Practice
1. a) The hen had several small, fluffy chicks.
   b) The pirate ship sank in the storm.
   c) The history book had an exciting cover.
   d) Patrick is the best swimmer in our class.
   e) The fearful dragon breathed green smoke from its nostrils.
2. a) Several small children came rushing towards us.
   b) Father Christmas was still wrapping the presents on Christmas Eve.
   c) Statues can be made from wood or stone.
   d) Tom couldn't find his puppy in the woods.
   e) Uncle John would have loved to go up in a hot air balloon.

Making sure
1-2. (*open*)

Practise your punctuation
1. a) A being from the Planet Astra landed in a spaceship.
   b) In December, the people of Scotland were terrified by a dragon.
   c) "Come quickly! I've found a box!" Jim shouted excitedly.
   d) The man called out in a loud voice, "Stop! Don't move!"
   e) Mrs Birch baked a cake but Billy's dog ate it.
   f) A strong wind blew through the trees.
2. (*open*)

Unit 15 Paragraphs

Focus
Introducing the concept of paragraphs

Definitions of terms used
A paragraph is a group of sentences that deals with one main idea or topic. A long piece of writing is easier to read if it is divided into paragraphs.

We begin a new paragraph by starting the first line a little way in from the margin. (This is called 'indenting'.)

Teacher's notes
Children will have come across paragraphs in their reading. Paragraphs make a text easier to read by breaking densely packed text into manageable sections. Like punctuation within sentences, paragraphing helps the reader understand the meaning.

Help children to see paragraphs in the hierarchy 'word - phrase - sentence - paragraph'.

Information books are often helpful in the study of paragraphs. Provide children with information texts to cut into paragraphs and discuss. Putting the text on a word processor allows children to experiment with it more easily.

The unit suggests indenting the first word of a new paragraph and starting a new line. This is particularly helpful when handwriting texts. There are other conventions that children could discuss, such as leaving a line between paragraphs.

There may be more than one correct way of dividing a text into paragraphs.

Answers
Practice
1. a) Angel Falls
   b) Niagara Falls
2. (*open*)

Making sure
1-3 (*open*)

Practise your punctuation
  Lakes result from the flow of water into low areas. Lake water comes largely from rainfall and melting snow. The water enters a lake basin through brooks, streams, rivers and underground springs.
  Sometimes, a lake is formed when the crater of an extinct volcano fills with water. Crater Lake in Oregon is an example of this.
  Lakes may also be artificially made. When a dam is built across a river valley, it will block the flow of water and form a lake. Lake Mead was formed when the Hoover Dam was built on the Colorado River.

Unit 16 Sentences (subject and verb agreement)

Focus
Extending children's understanding of subject and verb agreement

Definitions of terms used
Every sentence must have a subject and a verb. The verb must always agree with (match) the subject.

When the subject is singular, we must use the singular form of the verb with it. When the subject is plural, we must use the plural form of the verb with it.

Teacher's notes
An important rule of grammar is that the subject of a sentence must always agree with (match) the verb. Verb endings change according to whether the subject is singular or plural. The subject of a sentence may be just one noun, or it may be a noun phrase or a pronoun.

When writing, children often get carried away with their thoughts and lose sight of how a sentence began. This is one reason for encouraging them to reread their own work to make sure that it makes sense.

Book 3

Answers

Practice

1-2. (*open*)

3-4. a) Auntie Jane [s] likes [v] ice cream.
   b) The settee [s] needs [v] some soft cushions.
   c) The children [s] wear [v] jeans.
   d) The detective [s] solves [v] the mystery.
   e) Doctors [s] check [v] us to make sure we are healthy.
   f) The telephone [s] rings [v] loudly.
   g) Sharks [s] live [v] in the sea.

Making sure

1.

	to be (present tense)	to be (past tense)	to do (present tense)	to do (past tense)	to have (present tense)	to have (past tense)
I	am	was	do	did	have	had
you	are	were	do	did	have	had
he	is	was	does	did	has	had
she	is	was	does	did	has	had
it	is	was	does	did	has	had
we	are	were	do	did	have	had
you	are	were	do	did	have	had
they	are	were	do	did	have	had

2 a) Art is my favourite subject.
   b) The rowdy children were making a lot of noise.
   c) Were you late for school this morning?
   d) They weren't very good apples.
   e) I did it.
   f) Tom has a lot of work to do.

Practise your punctuation

1 a) Where is the car going?
   b) A fox lives in a home called a den.
   c) The boy does well at spelling, reading, maths and science.
   d) In the morning, the bus arrives here.
   e) The small girl, who has a dirty face, enjoys chocolate.
   f) The frog, which is large and fat, hops on to a rock.
   g) Hasn't the footballer scored yet ?

2 a) Where are the cars going?
   b) Foxes live in a home called a den.
   c) The boys do well at spelling, reading, maths and science.
   d) In the morning, the buses arrive here.
   e) The small girls, who have dirty faces, enjoy chocolate.
   f) The frogs, which are large and fat, hop on to a rock.
   g) Haven't the footballers scored yet ?

Unit 17 Prepositions

Focus

Extending children's understanding of prepositions

Definitions of terms used

A preposition is a word that tells us the position of one thing in relation to another.

Teacher's notes

The word **preposition** contains the word **position**. This should help children to remember the function of prepositions.

Demonstrate physically how prepositions work with objects in the classroom, using some of the prepositions introduced in the unit.

Some prepositions are linked with particular words, and this idea is explored in the unit. For example, it is correct to say 'different **from**', not 'different **to**'.

Answers

Practice

1. on – off, above – below, over – under, down – up, inside – outside, with – without, from – to

2 a) round
   b) up
   c) in
   d) off
   e) over
   f) on
   g) past

3. Here are some possible answers.
   a) The dog jumped (over, off, behind) the wall.
   b) A grey squirrel climbed (up, into) the oak tree.
   c) Emma wrote to her penfriend.
   d) The seal dived into the cold sea.
   e) A police helicopter flew (over, behind, past, near, between) the trees.
   f) I found my lost sock (under, on, in, by, near) the bed.
   g) The freight train pulled into the station.

Making sure

1. The shop was full of people.
2. Don't rely on me.
3. I agreed with the politician.
4. My coat is similar to yours.
5. I was ashamed of myself.
6. The boy protested against his punishment.
7. Apples are good for you.
8. Don't be angry with me.
9. Stuart was suffering from a bad cold.
10. I was guilty of telling a lie.
11. My shirt is different from yours.
12. Please wait for me.

Practise your punctuation

1-2. Did you know that mountain gorillas are found <u>in</u> Africa? They live <u>in</u> groups <u>in</u> the high mountain ranges. As they move <u>through</u> the forests, they search <u>for</u> fruit and roots.   Their movement depends <u>upon</u> the weather, but as a general rule they may travel <u>between</u> two and three miles a day. Gorillas live <u>on</u> the ground but the younger ones climb trees <u>after</u> fruit, sometimes throwing some of it down <u>to</u> the older members of the group.

58

Book 3

Unit 18 Clauses

Focus
Introducing the concept of clauses

Definitions of terms used
A clause is a group of words which can be used either as a whole sentence or as part of a sentence.

A clause must always contain a verb.

A simple one-clause sentence is always made up of two parts – a subject (who or what the sentence is about) and a predicate (the rest of the sentence).

Teacher's notes
At the beginning of the unit, revise what children have already learned about sentence structure and analysis:
- A sentence must have a subject and a verb.
- The subject must agree with the verb.
- A simple sentence is made up of a subject and a predicate (the rest of the sentence including the verb).

A clause consists of a subject and a predicate, and is a coherent unit of sense. A clause might, therefore, be the same as a simple sentence. This unit begins at this very basic level and then shows how two such sentences may be linked by a conjunction.

Answers

Practice

1-2. (*open*)

3.
   a) My best friend   came to tea.
   b) Curry   tastes very spicy.
   c) Our teacher   shouted at us.
   d) We   cycled all the way home.

Making sure

a) The girls fetched their bikes and went to the park.
b) The spider had eight legs and crawled slowly.
c) I love cauliflower but I do not like sprouts.
d) We set out early and had a good time.
e) I enjoy watching television but our television is broken.
f) We chose a pizza and ordered it from the waiter.
g) Tom scored full marks in spelling but he only got one sum correct.
h) The workman mixed the cement and tipped it into the hole.

Practise your punctuation

1.
   a) The lady went into the shop and bought a new dress.
   b) Tara shut the door but left the window open.
   c) We saw Manchester United play when we were visiting Uncle Paul.
   d) There were eight of us so we had to take two cars.
   e) The alsatian looked fierce but he was really quite tame.
   f) Tibs, my cat, is very fat and eats too much.

2.
   a) The lady went into the shop. She bought a new dress.
   b) Tara shut the door. She left the window open.
   c) We visited Uncle Paul. We saw Manchester United play.
   d) There were eight of us. We had to take two cars.
   e) The alsatian looked fierce. He was really quite tame.
   f) Tibs, my cat, is very fat. It eats too much.

Unit 19 Indirect Speech

Focus
Introducing the concept of indirect speech

Definitions of terms used
We can write speech in two ways – as direct speech or as indirect speech.

In direct speech, the speaker's exact words are enclosed in inverted commas.

In indirect speech, the speaker's exact words are not used, so inverted commas are not needed.

Teacher's notes
Indirect speech is a way of reporting what a person said without using the exact words spoken. This is why it is sometimes referred to as reported speech. Because the exact words are not used, inverted commas are not required.

Discuss the fact that indirect speech is frequently used in the media.

Draw attention to the fact that extensive changes may need to be made to the sentence construction when converting from direct to indirect speech (or *vice versa*). This applies especially to the positioning of the subject, to the verb tenses and to any pronouns.

Answers

Practice

1. Carl asked the old lady how old she was.
2. The doctor asked Mrs Williams to sit down.
3. The drowning man shouted for help and asked for someone to throw him a lifebelt.
4. The librarian asked Eve to take the book back to the shelves.
5. The king asked whether anyone had seen his crown.
6. The teacher looked at me and told me that I must learn my spellings.
7. Mark's mother asked him to get her some eggs from the shop.
8. Uncle John remarked that it was raining very heavily.
9. Dr Fisher told Jane that the pills would soon make her better.
10. The mechanic explained to Mr Jones that the brakes needed mending.

Making sure

1. "Have you hurt yourself, Marissa?" Mr Bertoli asked the girl.
2. The boy said, "I know the answer."
3. "I've lost my ring!" Mrs Azadi cried.
4. "I'll be eighty next year," the old man remarked.
5. "I've just found some money," Kerry told Gemma.
6. The teacher asked, "Why were you away last week, Ruth?"
7. "The house has been burgled," reported the police officer.
8. "I could easily climb that mountain," boasted the mountaineer.
9. "I am not guilty," protested the criminal.
10. "I will not buy you any new trainers!" exclaimed Sara's dad.

Practise your punctuation

1. Mr Parish: What's for tea tonight?
   Mrs Parish: Would you like curry, spaghetti, pizza or fish fingers?

Book 3

Mr Parish: I think I'd like hamburgers, please.
Mrs Parish: Just a minute! I didn't offer you hamburgers!
Mr Parish: I know, but they're what I really fancy.
Mrs Parish: Oh, well, you'll just have to cook them yourself!

2. Mr Parish asked his wife what was for tea that night. Mrs Parish said that he could have curry, spaghetti, pizza or fish fingers. Mr Parish replied that he would like hamburgers. Mrs Parish said that she had not offered him hamburgers. Mr Parish answered that they were what he really fancied. Mrs Parish said that he would just have to cook them himself.

Unit 20 Verb Tenses (future)

Focus
Introducing verbs written in the future tense, and revising the present and past tenses

Definitions of terms used
When we write verbs in the future tense, we often use the auxiliary verb **will** to help the main verb.

Teacher's notes
The tense of a verb tells us when something happens.

The most common way of expressing the future tense is to use the auxiliary verb **will**. To be perfectly correct, we should use **shall** after **I**, and **will** after **we, you, they, he, she** and **it**. However, in everyday language, **will** is most often used.

The future tense may also be expressed by using the verb **to go**.

Play a game in class. Have fun predicting the future. Write a set of 'predictions' on slips of paper and put them in a box: ' ... will live to a hundred.'; '... will play for England.'; '... will have sixteen children.' Children take it in turns to take a slip of paper and see what the future holds for them!

Answers

Practice

1. | Present tense | Future tense |
    | --- | --- |
    | a) Today I am riding a bike. | Tomorrow I will ride a bike. |
    | b) Today you are digging the garden. | Tomorrow you will dig the garden. |
    | c) Today he is doing maths. | Tomorrow he will do maths. |
    | d) Today she is going to school. | Tomorrow she will go to school. |

2. | Future tense | Past tense |
    | --- | --- |
    | a) Tomorrow she will come. | Yesterday she came. |
    | b) Tomorrow it will appear. | Yesterday it appeared. |
    | c) Tomorrow we will dance. | Yesterday we danced. |
    | d) Tomorrow they will play. | Yesterday they played. |

Making sure

1. | Present tense | Past tense | Future tense |
   | --- | --- | --- |
   | I sing | I sang | I will sing |
   | You eat | You ate | You will eat |
   | He washes | He washed | He will wash |
   | She likes | She liked | She will like |
   | It disappears | It disappeared | It will disappear |
   | We explain | We explained | We will explain |
   | I argue | I argued | I will argue |
   | We grow | We grew | We will grow |

2. I will get up at seven o'clock and have my breakfast. I will play football for half an hour and read my comic, and then I will call for my friend. We will walk to school and play in the playground. In the morning we will have Maths and English. At lunchtime I will have a jacket potato with cheese.

Practise your punctuation

1. On Wednesday, Sujata will run home from school and have a quick snack. She will get changed and go into town with her mum, Mrs Patel. They will look for a present for her sister Saima's birthday. After this, they will stay in town and choose Sujata a new skirt, jumper, coat and pair of shoes. What a busy evening it will be!

2. On Wednesday, Sujata ran home from school and had a quick snack. She got changed and went into town with her mum, Mrs Patel. They looked for a present for her sister Saima's birthday. After this, they stayed in town and chose Sujata a new skirt, jumper, coat and pair of shoes. What a busy evening it was!

Book 3

Progress Test B

Answers

1. a) <u>The hot air balloon</u> floated over (<u>open</u>).
   b) <u>The workman</u> picked up (<u>open</u>).
   c) <u>The old lady</u> was carrying (<u>open</u>).
   d) <u>A beautiful butterfly</u> landed on (<u>open</u>).

2. a) dog's
   b) Mrs Nelson's
   c) boys'
   d) mice's
   e) lady's
   f) birds'

3. a) I rode my bike to school.
   b) Mr Peek crashed his car.
   c) We realised that our tent was ripped.
   d) The children picked up their books.

4. a) The dog belongs to me. It is mine.
   b) Does this money belong to you? Is it yours?
   c) We bought the apples. They are ours.
   d) The boots belong to the footballers. They are theirs.

5 - 7. (*open*)

8. a) The chairs need painting.
   b) Plink and Plonk are cartoon characters.
   c) A line of cars was blocking the way.
   d) Uncle Steve did it.
   e) He doesn't play tennis very well.
   f) Each child has a packed lunch.
   g) All the oranges were bad.

9. a) full of
   b) share between
   c) similar to
   d) angry with
   e) according to
   f) wait for

10. a) <u>The children packed their bags</u> and <u>went home</u>.
    b) <u>The teacher was happy with Charlotte</u> but <u>she was cross with Khayyam</u>.
    c) <u>The driver braked hard</u> but <u>could not stop</u>.
    d) <u>Monkeys love eating bananas</u> and <u>like climbing trees</u>.

11. The pirate will row his boat to the island and jump on to the sand. He will unload the box of jewels and look for somewhere to hide it. He will search the whole island. The pirate will find a good spot in a cave and bury the treasure there.

12. a) The object of a sentence is the person or thing affected by the verb.
    b) A possessive noun always has an apostrophe in it.
    c) A possessive adjective describes who something belongs to.
    d) A phrase is a group of words which forms part of a sentence.
    e) A paragraph is a group of sentences that deal with one main idea.
    f) The subject of a sentence must always agree with the verb.
    g) A clause is a group of words which contains a verb; it can be used as a complete sentence, or part of a sentence.
    h) The future tense tells of something that will happen in the future.

Book 4

Unit	Content
1	Parts of Speech (nouns, adjectives, verbs, adverbs, pronouns and prepositions
2	Verbs (regular and irregular)
3	Verbs (transitive; active and passive)
4	Adverbs
5	Phrases (adjective and adverb)
6	Nouns (singular and plural)
7	Pronouns
8	Capital Letters
9	Direct Speech
10	Nouns (concrete and abstract)
	Progress Test A
11	Adjectives (prefixes and suffixes)
12	Clauses
13	Complex Sentences
14	Brackets and Hyphens
15	Paragraphs
16	Apostrophes (contractions and possessive nouns)
17	Standard English
18	Sentences (double negatives; subject and verb agreement)
19	Nouns (gender)
20	Shortening and Extending Sentences
	Progress Test B

Scope and sequence of skills

Unit	Title	Practice	Making sure	Practise your punctuation
1	**Parts of Speech (nouns, adjectives, verbs, adverbs, pronouns and prepositions)** Page 4	Identifying parts of speech in sentences	Composing sentences from given parts of speech	Capital letters, full stops, apostrophes, commas; reinforcing work on parts of speech
2	**Verbs (regular and irregular)** Page 6	Putting verbs into the past tense; identifying regular and irregular verbs	Writing simple past and past perfect tenses	Capital letters, full stops, commas, inverted commas, exclamation marks, question marks; reinforcing work on irregular verbs
3	**Verbs (transitive; active and passive)** Page 8	Matching subjects with transitive verbs and objects	Changing sentences from active to passive and *vice versa*	Capital letters, full stops, commas, apostrophes; identifying subject and verb
4	**Adverbs** Page 10	Writing opposites of adverbs of manner, time and place	Sentence completion using given compound adverbs	Capital letters, full stops, commas, exclamation marks, inverted commas, apostrophes; reinforcing work on adverbs
5	**Phrases (adjective and adverb)** Page 12	Sentence completion using given adjective and adverb phrases	Identifying adjective and adverb phrases	Capital letters, full stops, apostrophes; reinforcing work on phrases
6	**Nouns (singular and plural)** Page 14	Writing singular and plural forms of regular and irregular nouns	Writing singular and plural forms of irregular nouns	Capital letters, full stops, question marks, commas, inverted commas; reinforcing work on singular and plural and subject/verb agreement

Book 4

Unit	Title	Practice	Making sure	Practise your punctuation
7	**Pronouns** Page 16	Classifying pronouns into singular and plural	Classifying pronouns into first, second and third person (singular and plural)	Capital letters, full stops, commas, question marks, exclamation marks, apostrophes, inverted commas; reinforcing work on pronouns
8	**Capital Letters** Page 18	Identifying proper nouns	Using capital letters appropriately	Capital letters, full stops, apostrophes, commas; reinforcing work on capital letters
9	**Direct Speech** Page 20	Punctuating passages in direct speech	Punctuating passages in direct speech	Capital letters, full stops, commas, inverted commas, question marks; revising indirect speech; setting out dialogue as a play script.
10	**Nouns (concrete and abstract)** Page 22	Classifying concrete and abstract nouns; sentence completion	Identifying abstract nouns; changing adjectives into abstract nouns	Capital letters, full stops, commas; reinforcing work on abstract and concrete nouns
	Progress Test A Page 24	Revising and testing aspects of grammar taught in previous ten units		
11	**Adjectives (prefixes and suffixes)** Page 26	Adding prefixes to adjectives to form opposites; matching adjectives and definitions	Identifying root nouns in adjectives; making adjectives from nouns	Capital letters, full stops, commas, inverted commas, exclamation marks, apostrophes; reinforcing work on adjectives
12	**Clauses** Page 28	Compound sentences, using conjunctions; identifying clauses	Identifying main clauses; adding clauses to sentences	Capital letters, full stops, commas; reinforcing work on clauses
13	**Complex Sentences** Page 30	Matching main and subordinate clauses; adding subordinate clauses	Using **who** and **which**; sentence completion with subordinate clauses	Capital letters, full stops, commas; reinforcing work on clauses
14	**Brackets and Hyphens** Page 32	Using brackets	Identifying compound adjectives; forming compound adjectives	Capital letters, full stops, commas, apostrophes, question marks, exclamation marks, inverted commas, hyphens, brackets
15	**Paragraphs** Page 34	Sequencing paragraphs	Writing paragraphs from notes	Punctuation and paragraphing
16	**Apostrophes (contractions and possessive nouns)** Page 36	Contractions	Possessive nouns (singular and plural)	Capital letters, full stops, commas, apostrophes
17	**Standard English** Page 38	Putting sentences into Standard English vocabulary	Putting sentences into Standard English grammar	Capital letters, full stops, commas, question marks, exclamation marks, apostrophes, inverted commas; reinforcing work on Standard English

63

Book 4

Unit	Title	Practice	Making sure	Practise your punctuation
18	**Sentences (double negatives; subject and verb agreement)** Page 40	Correcting double negatives	Correcting sentences so that subject and verb agree	Capital letters, full stops, commas, question marks, exclamation marks, apostrophes, inverted commas; reinforcing work on double negatives, subject/verb agreement and Standard English
19	**Nouns (gender)** Page 42	Matching masculine and feminine nouns	Classifying nouns according to gender; identifying gender of nouns	Capital letters, full stops, commas, question marks, apostrophes, inverted commas, hyphens; reinforcing work on gender of nouns
20	**Shortening and Extending Sentences** Page 44	Shortening and extending sentences by omitting or adding various parts of speech	Extending sentences by adding phrases and clauses	Capital letters, full stops, commas, exclamation marks, apostrophes, inverted commas, hyphens
	Progress Test B Page 46	Revising and testing aspects of grammar taught in previous ten units		

Book 4

Unit 1 Parts of Speech (nouns, adjectives, verbs, adverbs, pronouns and prepositions)

Focus
Extending children's understanding of the concept of parts of speech

Definitions of terms used
Grammar is the study of the way in which we use words to make sentences. Words may be divided into groups called parts of speech (or word classes). Six important parts of speech are: nouns, adjectives, verbs, adverbs, pronouns and prepositions.

Teacher's notes
Begin the unit by reviewing and checking children's understanding of the six parts of speech. Explain that words can be divided into groups according to their function, or the way in which they are used in sentences. Parts of speech are sometimes called 'word classes'.

There are eight main parts of speech in English: nouns, adjectives, verbs, adverbs, prepositions, pronouns, conjunctions and articles. The term 'parts of speech' is slightly deceptive because these word groups are found in writing as well as in speech.

Answers
Practice

1 a) Jamal carefully placed the heavy case on the bed.
             adv   v   p

            adv   v   p
   b) Slowly the tortoise plodded under the hedge.
                      v   p   v
   c) Jemma looked at the floor and apologised
       adv   p
      tearfully to her teacher.
          adv   v   p
   d) Yesterday the girls went into town.
        p   adj   n
2 a) I tripped over the loose floorboard.
               p   adj   n
   b) Will she buy the most expensive dress?
                  adj   n   n p
   c) When the old man reached the bench he sat down.
           n   adj   p   p
   d) Cartoons are popular because they make us laugh.

Making sure
(open)

Practise your punctuation

1. There was a young man from Darjeeling
who travelled by bus into Ealing.
A man near the door
said, "Don't sit on the floor."
So he carefully sat on the ceiling.

2. a) man, Darjeeling, bus, Ealing, door, floor, ceiling
   b) young
   c) was, travelled, said, don't sit, sat
   d) carefully
   e) he
   f) from, by, near, on

Unit 2 Verbs (regular and irregular)

Focus
Developing the idea that many verbs have an irregular form in the past tense; introducing the past perfect tense which takes the auxiliary verb **to have**

Definitions of terms used
Some verbs are regular. This means that the main part of the verb (the root) stays the same when the tense changes.

Some verbs are irregular. This means that the root of the verb changes when the tense changes.

Teacher's notes
This unit deals with some irregular verbs in which the stem, or root, of the verb changes in the simple past tense: **wake** becomes **woke**, **catch** becomes **caught**. The past perfect tense, using the auxiliary verb **to have**, is introduced.

Answers
Practice

1-2 a) is – was i
     b) call – called r
     c) blow – blew i
     d) walk – walked r
     e) wash – washed r
     f) catch – caught i
     g) open – opened r
     h) feel – felt i
     i) miss – missed r
     j) invite – invited r
     k) find – found i
     l) bring – brought i
     m) cook – cooked r
     n) help – helped r
     o) write – wrote i

3-4 a) The driver <u>made</u> a mistake. i
     b) The waiter <u>poured</u> a drink. r
     c) We <u>gave</u> the cat some milk. i
     d) You <u>drank</u> a bottle of pop. i
     e) I <u>fell</u> over and <u>broke</u> my leg. i i
     f) The actor <u>performed</u> well. r
     g) She <u>celebrated</u> her birthday. r
     h) My mum <u>baked</u> some lovely cakes. r
     i) The child <u>shook</u> with cold. i

Making sure

Present tense (i)	Simple past tense	Past tense using **has** or **have**	Regular (r) or irregular
I drink	I drank	I have drunk	i
I speak	I spoke	I have spoken	i
I collect	I collected	I have collected	r
I skate	I skated	I have skated	r
I take	I took	I have taken	i
I do	I did	I have done	i
I nibble	I nibbled	I have nibbled	r
I steal	I stole	I have stolen	i
I know	I knew	I have known	i
I freeze	I froze	I have frozen	i

Practise your punctuation

1 a) When Will threw the stick, Fido, his pet dog, brought it back again.
   b) "Please, Miss, I have broken my pencil," Jane said.
   c) Abdi cried loudly, "Someone has taken my pencil!"
   d) On Thursday, Bill did his work well and wrote very neatly.
   e) Has Paula drawn many good pictures?
   f) Beth would have chosen a lolly but they were all sold.

65

Book 4

Unit 3 Verbs (transitive; active and passive)

Focus
Introducing the concept of transitive verbs and the concept of active and passive verbs

Definitions of terms used
Every sentence has a subject and a verb. Some sentences also have an object. The object is the person or thing affected by the verb. Verbs which take an object are called 'transitive' verbs.

A verb is active when the subject of the sentence does the action. A verb is passive when the subject of the sentence has the action done to it.

Teacher's notes
Introduce the unit by revising children's understanding of the concept of subject and verb, and the fact that every sentence must have a subject and a verb.

The unit deals with transitive verbs (verbs that take an object), and active and passive verbs.

Some verbs may be transitive or intransitive: 'I am playing tennis.' 'I am playing.'

Note how the subject and the object change position when a sentence is made passive.

Answers
Practice
1. The Romans invaded Britain.
2. Queen Victoria wore long dresses.
3. The angry bull chased the boy.
4. Farmer Giles ploughed his field.
5. The young princess married a foreign prince.
6. Squirrels eat nuts.
7. The tennis player hit the ball.

Making sure
1. a) The city was surrounded by mighty walls.
   b) First prize in the raffle was won by Mr Azadi.
   c) The dragon was killed by St George.
   d) The stranded mountaineer was rescued by the helicopter.
   e) A clever plan was devised by the officer in charge.
   f) The merchant ship was boarded by some fierce pirates.
   g) The computer was switched on by Amy.
   h) The telephone was picked up by the shop assistant.
2. a) The doctor examined Mrs Baker.
   b) The soldiers opened the city gates.
   c) A group of older children bullied the small boy.
   d) Rumpelstiltskin locked the princess in the tower.
   e) Mr Fensome hung out the washing to dry.
   f) The pop star performed a new song.
   g) Emperor Caligula rode the white stallion.

Practise your punctuation
1-2 a) The President of the United States (summoned) his advisers.
   b) The gold medal (was won) by China.
   c) Roald Dahl (wrote) many children's books.
   d) The jagged rock (tore) Pedro's shirt.
   e) The chocolates, sweets, crisps and cakes (were eaten) by the hungry children.
   f) Smudge, my pet dog, (ate) the big, juicy bone.

Unit 4 Adverbs

Focus
Revising and extending children's understanding of adverbs of manner, time and place

Definitions of terms used
An adverb is a word which gives more meaning to a verb.
An adverb of manner tells us how something happened.
An adverb of time tells us when something happened.
An adverb of place tells us where something happened.

Teacher's notes
There are three kinds of adverb: adverbs of manner (**brightly**, **quickly**); adverbs of time (**now**, **then**, **always**); adverbs of place (**here**, **there**). Adverbs of time are useful for writing instructions, and adverbs of place are often used in written or spoken directions.

Answers
Practice
1. a) gently – roughly
   b) quietly – loudly (noisily)
   c) happily – sadly (unhappily)
   d) jerkily – smoothly
   e) carefully – carelessly
2. a) lastly – first (firstly)
   b) afterwards – before
   c) tomorrow – yesterday
   d) earlier – later
   e) now – then
3. a) somewhere – nowhere
   b) inside – outside
   c) forwards – backwards
   d) here – there
   e) downwards – upwards

Making sure
1. Our teacher told us not to talk so loudly.
2. The old lady fell rather heavily.
3. We tried really hard to win the game.
4. Kylie almost always chooses chips for tea.
5. After I was told off, I tried much harder with my writing.
6. The thirsty dog drank the milk quite noisily.
7. Sara did her spellings very badly. She did less well than last week.
8. James smiles more often than I do but Kirsty smiles most often.

Practise your punctuation
1-2 a) Lions <u>seldom</u> drink at the same place <u>twice</u>.
   b) "Slow <u>down</u>. Don't walk so <u>quickly</u>," grumbled old Mr Saunders.
   c) Donna waited <u>very patiently</u> in the queue for the singer's autograph.
   d) "You've done <u>quite well</u>, Mark!" exclaimed Mrs Francis. "However, I think you can try <u>even harder</u>."
   e) After the explosion, the house collapsed <u>very quickly</u>.
   f) The stamp collector said, "You <u>very rarely</u> see a stamp from Iceland <u>today</u>."

Unit 5 Phrases (adjective and adverb)

Focus
Introducing adjective and adverb phrases

Book 4

Definitions of terms used

Sometimes we need a phrase instead of an adjective or an adverb.

A phrase which tells us more about a noun is an adjective phrase.

A phrase which tells us more about a verb is an adverb phrase.

Teacher's notes

Note how commas are often used to separate phrases in order to make the meaning clearer.

Answers

Practice

1. a) The lady was carrying a bag, full of shopping.
   b) Long and white, the old man's beard nearly reached the floor.
   c) The castle, with its high, grey walls, looked rather frightening.
   d) The large room was cold and draughty.
   e) The giant, taller than a house, stamped his foot angrily.
2. a) They went home after tea.
   b) We played rounders on the school field.
   c) We sat, quietly and attentively, listening to the story.
   d) The lion pounced, as quick as a flash.
   e) Raza wrote his story carelessly and untidily.

Making sure

1. a) The sheep, <u>glad to be out of doors</u>, were grazing in the field.
   b) The apples, <u>fresh and crisp</u>, were from New Zealand.
   c) The boy stopped suddenly, <u>filled with fear</u>.
   d) <u>Heavy and solid</u>, the door creaked noisily as we pushed it open.
   e) We chose the chair <u>with the comfortable cushions</u>.
2. a) The sheep were glad to be out of doors. They were grazing in the field.
   b) The apples were fresh and crisp. They were from New Zealand.
   c) The boy stopped suddenly. He was filled with fear.
   d) The door was heavy and solid. It creaked noisily as we pushed it open.
   e) We chose a chair. It had comfortable cushions.
3. a) <u>Every Friday</u> we buy fish and chips. (when)
   b) Tim coloured the picture <u>as carefully as possible</u>. (how)
   c) <u>With a great effort</u>, Mrs Lacey lifted the heavy case. (how)
   d) The bird flew, <u>slowly but gracefully</u>, on to the top branch of the tree. (how)
   e) The lion disappeared, <u>merging into the background</u>. (where)

Practise your punctuation

1. a) The farmer looked at the sky. It was cloudy and overcast.
   b) Harry's jeans were new. They came from the United States.
   c) They crept through the forest. They moved stealthily and quietly.
   d) Jane's sister held her hand to cross the road. Her sister was older and more sensible.

2. a) The farmer looked up at the <u>cloudy and overcast</u> sky. (adjective phrase)
   b) Harry's jeans, <u>new and fashionable</u>, were from the United States. (adjective phrase)
   c) They crept through the forest, moving <u>stealthily and quietly</u>. (adverb phrase)
   d) Jane's sister, <u>older and more sensible</u>, held Jane's hand to cross the road. (adjective phrase)

Unit 6   Nouns (singular and plural)

Focus

Revising regular singular and plural nouns and introducing some irregular ones

Definitions of terms used

Most nouns may be written in either the singular (one) or the plural (more than one). Most nouns follow rules for making the plural form.

Teacher's notes

This unit deals with the rules for pluralising regular singular nouns. Some irregular plurals are also introduced.

Use the unit to reinforce the point that subjects and verb must always agree.

Answers

Practice

1. a) emperor – emperors
   b) skill – skills
   c) life – lives
   d) body – bodies
   e) ash – ashes
   f) wife – wives
   g) watch – watches
   h) dish – dishes
   i) country – countries
   j) loaf – loaves
   k) wolf – wolves
   l) fly – flies
2. a) cities – city
   b) seeds – seed
   c) monkeys – monkey
   d) shelves – shelf
   e) thieves – thief
   f) foxes – fox
   g) brothers – brother
   h) impurities – impurity
   i) wishes – wish
   j) dresses – dress
   k) halves – half
   l) factories – factory
3. a) Poppies are lovely flowers.
   b) The boys wrote in the diaries.
   c) The foxes hid in the bushes.
   d) The ladies put the loaves on the shelves.
   e) The girls played with the babies and then tried on the dresses.

Making sure

1. a) ox – oxen
   b) fish – fish
   c) deer – deer
   d) foot – feet
   e) goose – geese
   f) mouse – mice
   g) sheep – sheep
   h) man – men
   i) child – children

67

Book 4

2. *Nouns which change in unexpected ways in the plural*
   ox
   oot
   goose
   mouse
   man
   child

   Nouns which don't change at all in the plural
   fish
   deer
   sheep

Practise your punctuation
1. a) A lady played with her baby on the grass.
   b) The boy picked up the knife and cut the berry from the branch.
   c) "Will you need scissors and pliers to make the toy?" the teacher asked the girl.
   d) The workman promised to mend the hole in the roof.
   e) "Buy some new trousers, pants, jeans and shorts," the woman said to the child.
   f) The fox could see that the fish was swimming in the pond near the bush.
2. a) Some ladies played with their babies on the grass.
   b) The boys picked up the knives and cut the berries from the branches.
   c) "Will you need scissors and pliers to make the toys?" the teachers asked the girls.
   d) The workmen promised to mend the holes in the roofs.
   e) "Buy some new trousers, pants, jeans and shorts," the women said to the children.
   f) The foxes could see that the fish were swimming in the ponds near the bushes.

Unit 7   Pronouns

Focus
Extending children's understanding of singular and plural pronouns

Definitions of terms used
Sometimes when we are talking about people or things we use pronouns instead of nouns. Pronouns may be singular (one person or thing). Pronouns may be plural (more than one person or thing). The pronoun **you** may be singular or plural.

Teacher's notes
The prefix **pro** literally means 'in the place of', and so **pronoun** means 'in the place of a noun'.

Pronouns help to avoid too much repetition. They are used extensively in spoken language when the person or thing being referred to is obvious or visible.

This unit covers personal (**I**), possessive (**mine**) and reflexive (**myself**) pronouns. It also classifies pronouns as first, second or third person.

Answers
Practice
1. *Singular pronouns*
   I
   he
   you
   me
   she
   it
   him
   her

   Plural pronouns
   you
   they
   us
   them
   we

2. a) she, her
   b) he, him
   c) it

Making sure

	Singular pronouns	Plural pronouns
First person	I, me, mine	we, us, ours
Second person	you, yourself	you, yourselves
Third person	he, she, it, him, hers	they, them, theirs, themselves

Practise your punctuation
1-2 a) "I suppose you think you're funny," the teacher said to Emma.
   b) "Stop spoiling our game! Leave us alone!" Fatima and Chloe shouted at Darren.
   c) "Is this your pen?" Mrs Harris asked. "Yes, I think it is mine," replied Mustafa.
   d) Chandrika and Carra were being teased by two big boys. They were calling them names.

Note
Our and **your** are called possessive adjectives in Book 3, but they may also be classified as pronouns.

Unit 8   Capital Letters

Focus
Using capital letters

Definitions of terms used
There are various uses for capital letters, apart from beginning sentences, beginning new lines in a poem and using the pronoun **I**.

Capital letters are used to begin: people's titles, initials and names; holy names; the names of months, days of the week and special days; the names of countries, towns and streets; adjectives made from the names of countries; the names of rivers, mountains and seas; the names of buildings; the names of companies and products; important words in the titles of books, films and television programmes; some abbreviations.

Teacher's notes
Revise children's existing knowledge of the use of capital letters.

Discuss the list of usages and expand on any which are unfamiliar.

In book and programme titles, it is usually only the important words that begin with capital letters.

Answers
Practice
1. mountain
2. Tuesday
3. Tower Bridge
4. Sweden
5. month

6. British Gas
7. Humpty Dumpty
8. Dutch
9. Kent
10. measles
11. Bristol
12. film
13. Saint Peter
14. city
15. the Mississippi
16. George Street
17. Queen Mary
18. Easter

Making sure
1. a) The Lion, the Witch and the Wardrobe
   b) Black Beauty
   c) Treasure Island
   d) Charlie and the Chocolate Factory
   e) Gulliver's Travels
   f) The Wizard of Oz
2. 3.30 p.m. Playdays
   3.50 p.m. Monster Movies
   4.05 p.m. The New Yogi Bear Show
   5.00 p.m. Newsround
   5.10 p.m. Blue Peter
3. a) Member of Parliament - MP
   b) On Her Majesty's Service - OHMS
   c) Prime Minister - PM
   d) United States of America - USA
   e) British Broadcasting Corporation - BBC
   f) Her Majesty's Ship - HMS

Practise your punctuation
1. The Houses of Parliament are near Big Ben in London.
2. Uncle Dave's birthday is on 8th November.
3. Argentina, Brazil, Colombia and Peru are countries in South America.
4. Last July I visited Italy on holiday. I stayed at the Dolce Vita Hotel.
5. Mr and Mrs Broom went to see the film called "The Lost Ark" at the Odeon Cinema in Leeds.
6. Ben Nevis is a mountain in Scotland.

Unit 9   Direct Speech

Focus
Introducing three different patterns for setting out direct speech

Definitions of terms used
When we write down someone's exact words, we call it 'direct speech'. We use inverted commas (speech marks) to mark the beginning and end of what the person says. Whenever a new person starts speaking, we start a new line.

Teacher's notes
Three different patterns for setting out direct speech are introduced in this unit, providing the potential for variety in setting down dialogue when writing.

Children need to be reminded that: everything the person says goes inside the inverted commas; a new line should be started every time a new person speaks; a capital letter is used to begin the opening word of a speech (as this is really the beginning of the sentence being spoken); the spoken words should be separated from the reporting clause (the words which tell the reader who is speaking).

Answers
Practice
1. "Is something the matter?" asked Peter.
   " Don't worry. Everything is fine," replied Mrs Brown.
   " I hope Dad won't be away too long," said Roberta.
   " He should be back soon," answered Mrs Brown.
2. Mrs Brown said to the children, "It's time for bed."
   Peter begged, "Can't we stay up a bit longer?"
   Mrs Brown replied with a smile, "I'm afraid it's already past your bedtime."
   As she went upstairs, Roberta called, "Goodnight, Mum. I'll see you in the morning."

Making sure
"I'm afraid I've had some bad news," Mrs Brown said to the children. "Your father has had an accident."
"What's the matter?" Roberta asked. "Is it serious?"
"Will he have to go to hospital?" Peter asked. "Will he have to have an operation?"
"Now, don't worry," Mrs Brown replied. "It's not as bad as that. Someone crashed into his car, but he hasn't broken any bones."
"That's a relief!" Roberta exclaimed. "But I bet he's a bit shaken up!"
"He sounded fine on the telephone," Mrs Brown said, "but the car is badly damaged."
"A damaged car," said Peter, "is better than a damaged Dad!"

Practise your punctuation
1. Mr Brown asked the salesman how much the new car was. The salesman asked Mr Brown whether he had an old car to trade in. Mr Brown replied that he had just had an accident and that his car had been badly damaged. The salesman told him that didn't matter as he was sure they could agree on a good price. Mr Brown asked if he could go for a test run in the new car to try it out. The salesman agreed, but told him to take care, because one smashed car was enough!
2. (Answers may vary slightly)

Mr Brown:	How much is that new car?
Salesman:	Do you have an old car to trade in?
Mr Brown:	I have just had an accident. My old car was badly damaged.
Salesman:	That doesn't matter. I'm sure we can agree on a good price.
Mr Brown:	May I go for a test run in the new car to try it out?
Salesman:	Yes, but take care. One smashed car is enough!

Unit 10   Nouns (concrete and abstract)

Focus
Introducing the concept of concrete and abstract nouns

Definitions of terms used
Concrete nouns are the names of things which exist outside your mind. You can touch, taste, see, hear or smell these things.

Abstract nouns are nouns which represent thoughts, ideas and feelings. You cannot touch, taste, see, hear or smell these things.

69

Book 4

Teacher's notes

Revise children's existing knowledge of nouns.
Abstract nouns are more difficult to grasp than concrete nouns. Rather than spending time explaining the difference, work through the unit and then review children's understanding at the end.

Answers

Practice

1. *Concrete nouns*
   bread
   caravan
   pen
   door
   computer

   Abstract nouns
   honesty
   emptiness
   wonder
   beauty
   belief

2. a) The giant had the strength of ten men.
   b) The little people were terrified and looked at the giant with fear.
   c) The speed of the car was amazing.
   d) There is danger in climbing mountains.
   e) The cook was filled with anger when she saw the mess in the kitchen.
   f) The beggar lived in poverty.

Making sure

1. a) The old man had great <u>patience</u>.
   b) There was <u>love</u> in the eyes of the mother when she held her new baby.
   c) Louise looked at her present in <u>astonishment</u>.
   d) The <u>beauty</u> of the mountains was incredible.
   e) If you could have one <u>wish</u>, what would it be?
   f) The explorer showed <u>courage</u> when she was attacked by a wild bear.

2. a) sick – sickness
   b) ugly – ugliness
   c) dark – darkness
   d) dangerous – danger
   e) hot – heat
   f) joyful – joy
   g) foolish – foolishness
   h) silly – silliness
   i) high – height
   j) wealthy – wealth

3. (open)

Practise your punctuation

1-2 a) When <u>Mrs Grant</u>(c) confronted the <u>thief</u>(c), she saw <u>fear</u>(a) in his <u>eyes</u>(c).
   b) The <u>judge</u>(c), who had a long, white <u>beard</u>(c), praised the <u>witness</u>(c) for her <u>honesty</u>(a).
   c) The <u>funfair</u>(c) caused great <u>excitement</u>(a) when it came to <u>Bradford</u>(c).
   d) <u>Mr Younnas</u>(c) was filled with <u>happiness</u>(a) when he won the <u>Lottery</u>(c).
   e) Blinking and stumbling, I was blinded by the <u>brightness</u>(a) of the <u>torch</u>(c).
   f) My <u>grandad</u>(c) used to spend <u>hours</u>(a) playing with me. I was amazed at his <u>patience</u>(a).

Progress Test A

Answers

1. a) find – found i
   b) wonder – wondered r
   c) drink – drank i
   d) see – saw i
   e) refuse – refused r
   f) decide – decided r
   g) take – took i
   h) hug – hugged r
   i) defeat – defeated r
   j) teach – taught i

2. a) I have flown in a helicopter.
   b) The workers have built a big house.
   c) The spectators have all left the stadium.
   d) If I had shouted louder they would have heard me.
   e) The baby had only just woken up.

3. *Nouns*
   car
   house
   telephone
   (cold)

   Adjectives
   huge
   cold
   empty

   Verbs
   ran
   ate
   looked

   Adverbs
   slowly
   quietly
   greedily

   Pronouns
   he
   they
   us

   Prepositions
   in
   under
   behind

4. a) <u>The cricketer</u>(s) preferred(v) <u>his new bat</u>(o).
   b) <u>The famous opera singer</u>(s) sang(v) <u>a lovely song</u>(o).
   c) <u>The ball</u>(s) broke(v) <u>the window</u>(v).
   d) <u>The old man</u>(s) peeled(v) <u>the rosy, red apple</u>(o).

70

Book 4

e) <u>The old lady</u> knitted a <u>woolly jumper</u>.
     s   v   o

5. a) The new bat was preferred by the cricketer.
   b) A lovely song was sung by the famous opera singer.
   c) The window was broken by the ball.
   d) The rosy, red apple was peeled by the old man.
   e) A woolly jumper was knitted by the old lady.

6. a) wearily   m
   b) upwards   p
   c) later   t
   d) before   t
   e) cautiously m
   f) there   p
   g) narrowly m
   h) yesterday t
   i) backwards p
   j) loudly   m

7. (*open*)

8. The <u>hot and sticky</u> baby played ⟨in the bath⟩

9. a) half – halves
   b) church – churches
   c) city – cities
   e) mouse – mice
   f) rat – rats
   g) dress – dresses
   h) sheep – sheep
   i) knife – knives
   j) child – children
   k) calf – calves
   l) box – boxes

10. a) France
    b) Snow White
    c) title
    d) Jesus
    e) Oxford Street
    f) American
    g) computer
    h) Canterbury
    i) Mars
    j) Big Ben

11. *Concrete nouns*
    lamp
    potato
    grass
    bird
    shoe

    Abstract nouns
    truth
    justice
    speed
    courage

12.   s   p
    Emma and <u>I</u> climbed the tree. <u>We</u> saw a squirrel.
    s
    <u>It</u> ran along the branch and joined some other
                      p   p
    squirrels. <u>They</u> took no notice of <u>us</u>. Emma slipped.
     s   s
    <u>She</u> grabbed the branch tightly. "<u>You</u> had a narrow
            s
    escape," <u>I</u> laughed.

Unit 11 Adjectives (prefixes and suffixes)

Focus
Adding prefixes to the beginning of some adjectives to give them the opposite meaning; adding suffixes to the end of some nouns to change them into adjectives

Definitions of terms used
Prefixes can be placed at the beginning of some adjectives to give them the opposite meaning.

Suffixes can be placed at the end of some nouns to turn them into adjectives.

Teacher's notes
A prefix is a group of letters added to the beginning of a word to change its meaning. Some prefixes, such as **in** and **im**, give adjectives the opposite meaning.

Children will have come across suffixes before, although they will not necessarily know the term. Suffixes are used: to change a word from one part of speech to another (**bright - brightness**); to show how nouns, adjectives and verbs inflect (change to fit the grammar of the sentence).

This unit concentrates on the first usage. Allow children to use dictionaries to check their answers.

Answers
Practice
1. a) expensive – inexpensive
   b) patient – impatient
   c) proper – improper
   d) formal – informal
   e) sane – insane
   f) mortal – immortal
   g) mature – immature
   h) attentive – inattentive
   i) secure – insecure
   j) possible – impossible
   k) perfect – imperfect
   l) definite – indefinite
   m) pure – impure
   n) complete – incomplete
   o) practical – impractical

2. a) invisible – cannot be seen
   b) impassable – cannot be passed
   c) imperfect – not perfect
   d) indistinct – not clear
   e) incomplete – not complete
   f) inedible – not good to eat
   g) immovable – cannot be moved
   h) impure – not pure

Making sure
1. a) girlish – girl
   b) athletic – athlete
   c) sunny – sun
   d) volcanic – volcano
   e) childish – child
   f) watery – water
   g) energetic – energy
   h) faulty – fault
   i) gigantic – giant
   j) foolish – fool
   k) angry – anger
   l) boyish – boy

2. a) girlish, childish, foolish, boyish
   b) athletic, volcanic, energetic, gigantic
   c) sunny, watery, faulty, angry

71

Book 4

3.
   a) music – musical
   b) adventure – adventurous
   c) comfort – comfortable
   d) fashion – fashionable
   e) fame – famous
   f) accident – accidental
   g) value – valuable
   h) poison – poisonous
   i) nature – natural
   j) centre – central
   k) danger – dangerous
   l) misery – miserable

4. (open)

Practise your punctuation

1-2. Jane and Shahdad, two <u>British</u> mountaineers, had decided to do something <u>adventurous</u> and <u>energetic</u>. They attempted an almost <u>impossible</u> challenge, to climb Mount Kilimanjaro.

"What a <u>marvellous</u> view!" exclaimed Jane as she looked down at the valley below.

"It's a pity the summit is so <u>indistinct</u>," replied Shadad, looking up at the cloud-covered peak. Later, they reached an obstacle that was <u>impossible</u> to get past. As they were moving along a narrow, windswept ledge, Jane turned and said, "A huge boulder has made the ledge <u>impassable</u>. I'm afraid it's too <u>dangerous</u> to go on. We'll have to go down again."

Unit 12 Clauses

Focus
Single-clause sentences; two-clause sentences joined with a conjunction; main clauses

Definitions of terms used
A clause is a group of words which can be used either as a whole sentence or as part of a sentence. A clause always contains a verb.

We can make a two-clause sentence by joining the single-clause sentences with a conjunction.
(Conjunctions are sometimes called connectives.)

Teacher's notes
The concept of clauses was introduced in Unit 18 of Book 3. In this unit, the concept is extended to two-clause sentences.

Children frequently use multi-clause sentences in speech, and it is instructive to help them to understand the basics of sentence construction. However, an in-depth study at this level is unnecessary and inappropriate. This unit and Unit 13 have therefore been kept as simple as possible.

This unit deals with compound sentences, in which two main clauses are linked by a conjunction such as **and** or **but**.

Answers
Practice

1.
   a) The giant looked frightening but he was friendly.
   b) The giant walked up to Sophie and put his case down.
   c) The case was small but it was very heavy.
   d) Sophie looked up at the giant and smiled at him.
   e) It was a sunny day but dark clouds were beginning to gather.

2-3.
   a) <u>The giant jumped into the air</u> ⓐⓝⓓ <u>swung the net</u>.
   b) <u>He caught something in the net</u> ⓐⓝⓓ <u>laughed excitedly</u>.
   c) <u>Sophie picked up the jar</u> ⓐⓝⓓ <u>held it up for the giant</u>.
   d) <u>The giant tipped something into the jar</u> ⓐⓝⓓ <u>screwed on the lid</u>.
   e) <u>He held the jar close to his ear</u> ⓑⓤⓣ <u>heard nothing</u>.

Making sure

1.
   a) <u>Sophie was friends with the giant</u> although she was a little scared of him.
   b) <u>The night was dark</u> so it was difficult to see.
   c) <u>I played with my friend</u> after I had eaten my tea.
   d) <u>The frog was irritating</u> because it croaked so much.
   e) <u>The kangaroo hopped away</u> when the snake hissed at it.

2. (open)

Practise your punctuation

1.
   a) <u>The Odeon Theatre was full</u> because Gary Gold was so popular.
   b) When Gary came on to the stage, <u>the audience roared</u>.
   c) <u>Gary sang his latest song</u> after a fan requested it.
   d) Although the band played loudly, <u>no one complained</u>.
   e) Although he was tired, <u>Gary put everything into his act</u>.
   f) <u>Gary signed autographs</u> after the show had finished.

2. There may be same variation in the answers given.
   a) Because Gary was so popular, the Odeon Theatre was full.
   b) The audience roared when Gary came on to the stage.
   c) After a fan requested it, Gary sang his latest song.
   d) No one complained, although the band played loudly.
   e) Gary put everything into his act, although he was tired.
   f) After the show had finished, Gary signed autographs.

Unit 13 Complex Sentences

Focus
Main and subordinate clauses; complex sentences

Definitions of terms used
Every sentence contains at least one main (most important) clause.

A complex sentence contains one main clause and one or more subordinate (less important) clauses.

A main clause can be used on its own as a sentence.
A subordinate clause does not make sense on its own.

Teacher's notes
There are two kinds of multi-clause sentence:
- a compound sentence, in which two main clauses are linked by a conjunction

- a complex sentence, which consists of a main clause and one or more subordinate (or less important) clauses.

A main clause always makes sense by itself and can stand alone. Subordinate clauses add meaning to the main clause. They cannot stand alone, as they are dependent on the main clause.

Note

A subordinate clause introduced by **who** or **which** is not preceded by a comma if the pronoun is defining the subject of the sentence.

See 'Making sure' 1a), c), 2a); 'Practise your punctuation' 1-2a), d).

Answers

Practice

1. Everyone started talking as soon as the teacher left the room.
   Clouds form when water vapour in the air cools.
   The flowers did not grow although I watered them regularly.
   The rabbit escaped because the hutch door was left open.
   Children are not admitted unless they are with their parents.
   I visited Rome where I saw the Pope.
2. (*open*)

Making sure

1. a) I found the key which opens the old box.
   b) Emma wrote to her uncle, who sent her a present.
   c) Amir is the boy who won first prize.
   d) The police officer caught the thief, who had run away.
   e) I found the missing bag, which had been lost.
2. a) The girl who had stolen the money was punished by her mother.
   b) The old boat, which had a hole in it, sank in the lake.
   c) Emma, who had hurt her toe, was limping badly.
   d) The bird, which was singing loudly, was a lark.
   e) The thin dog, which was starving, gobbled up all the food.

Practise your punctuation

1-2 a) PC Sharp arrested the man who had robbed the bank in Runcorn Road.
   b) Sharon bought a magazine, which was full of pictures of her favourite band.
   c) Robin Hood, who was an outlaw, lived in Sherwood Forest.
   d) The man who invented television was called John Logie Baird.
   e) Mr Cusack praised Jamie, who had tried very hard at English.

Unit 14 Brackets and Hyphens

Focus

Introducing the concept of brackets and the concept of hyphens

Definitions of terms used

Brackets are punctuation marks which enclose information to show that it is separate from everything around it.

A hyphen is used when we join two words to make a compound adjective.

Book 4

Teacher's notes

Brackets are used in a similar way to a pair of commas, to enclose parts of a sentence which contain extra explanation or detail.

A hyphen is used to hold a pair of words together to help to make their meaning clear (as in the adjective **hard-working**). Another use for a hyphen (not explored in this unit) is at the end of a line when a word doesn't quite fit and has to be continued on the line below.

Answers

Practice

1. a) The puppies were playing when Mr Smith came in. They were rolling around the floor as usual.
   b) Brackets are useful punctuation marks. They are often used in a similar way to a pair of commas.
   c) Tower Bridge is quite an old bridge. It opens up to let ships pass along the river.
   d) Police officers get their nicknames from Sir Robert Peel. They are sometimes called "bobbies" or "peelers".
   e) The shoes were very expensive. They were made from the best leather.
2. a) The picture (shown on page 7) is of an aeroplane landing.
   b) Commas (like brackets) are often used in pairs.
   c) You will find ants practically everywhere (except on the summits of very high mountains).
   e) When a liquid evaporates (changes into a gas) it draws off heat.
   f) If you eat a balanced diet you will get all the vitamins you need (with the possible exception of Vitamin D).

Making sure

1. a) clean-shaven
   b) house-trained
   c) man-eating
   d) football-mad
   e) sweet-tasting
2. a) Someone who is mean is tight-fisted.
   b) Someone who steals is light-fingered.
   c) Someone showing surprise might be wide-eyed.
   d) Someone who is nervous may be tongue-tied.
   e) Someone who loves dogs is animal-loving.

Practise your punctuation

1. Ben, Sam's floppy-eared dog, was barking.
2. The monster with the flashing blue-green eyes ate anything it could find.
3. "Do you know the way to Norwich?" asked the stranger as he parked his car (a blue hatchback).
4. "Don't touch that button!" shouted the worried-looking mother. "It might be dangerous."
5. Much of London (including St Paul's Cathedral) was destroyed in the Great Fire, which happened in 1666.

Unit 15 Paragraphs

Focus

Extending children's understanding of paragraphs

Definitions of terms used

A paragraph is a group of sentences that deals with one main idea or topic. A long piece of writing is easier to read if it is divided into paragraphs.

We open a new paragraph by beginning the first line a little

73

Book 4

way in from the margin. (This is called 'indenting'.)

Teacher's notes
This unit builds on the work in Unit 15 of Book 3.

Answers
Practice

Remains of the oldest known baths have been discovered on Crete. They are thought tp be 4000 years old. There are footbaths and a very modern-looking tub.

In ancient times, the Greeks bathed in tubs made of polished stone. We know this because remains of such tubs have been found. Homer, a Greek poet, describes a beautiful silver tub in one of his poems.

By the Middle Ages, attitudes had changed. People rarely bathed at all. There were few private baths in homes. Many people used perfumes and cosmetics as a substitute for bathing to cover up any unpleasant smells.

It was not until Victorian times that bathrooms began to evolve as separate rooms in houses. The tub, made of wood, copper or iron, often had a cover over it to make it look like a sofa.

Making sure

1-2. (*open*)

Practise your punctuation

Moles are found mainly in Europe. They spend most of their time underground, digging complicated systems of tunnels and chambers. The soil they dig up appears on the surface as molehills.

The appearance of moles is distinctive. Moles' fur is soft, like black velvet. Their front paws, large and powerful, are specially designed for digging. Their small eyes are nearly hidden by their fur. In fact, moles are virtually blind.

Moles have an enormous appetite and seem to be constantly hungry. The mole's diet consists chiefly of earthworms. A mole will eat up to its own weight of earthworms in a day. They also eat larvae, but will eat almost any animal matter.

Unit 16 Apostrophes (contractions and possessive nouns)

Focus
Revising apostrophes

Definitions of terms used
There are two occasions when you should use an apostrophe:
- in a contraction (when two words are joined together and some letters are missed out)
- to show ownership

When there is just one owner, we usually add **'s** to the noun. ('the **boy's** bike')

When there are more than one owner, we add **'** to the noun if it ends in **s**. ('the **girls'** skateboards')

We add **'s** if there is no **s** at the end of the noun. ('the **children's** skates')

Teacher's notes
Discuss the explanations on page 37.

Answers
Practice

1. a) I'm – I am
   b) I've – I have
   c) she's – she is
   d) you're – you are
   e) it's – it is
   f) haven't – have not
   g) couldn't – could not
   h) wasn't – was not
   i) aren't – are not
   j) who's – who is
   k) we're – we are
   l) let's – let us
   m) they've – they have
   n) she'll – she will
   o) we'd – we had

2. a) I hadn't seen the film before.
   b) He didn't want it.
   c) That's a good book.
   d) We'll help.
   e) You'll be sorry.
   f) Don't go.
   g) It's a good idea.
   h) You shouldn't come.
   i) They're late.
   j) It wouldn't matter.
   k) We've got two.
   l) You needn't go in.

Making sure

a) the hat of the clown – the clown's hat
b) the antlers of the biggest deer – the biggest deer's antlers
c) the watch of the nurse – the nurse's watch
d) the shell of the tortoise – the tortoise's shell
e) the tail of the tiger – the tiger's tail
f) the claws of the cat – the cat's claws
g) the bike of my friend – my friend's bike

2. a) the whiskers of the cats – the cats' whiskers
   b) the eggs of the birds – the birds' eggs
   c) the den of the wolves – the wolves' den
   d) the tools of the workmen – the workmen's tools
   e) the wool of the sheep – the sheep's wool
   f) the club of the children – the children's club
   g) the paws of the dogs – the dogs' paws
   h) the manes of the lions – the lions' manes
   i) the uniforms of the men – the men's uniforms

3. a) The motorist's leg was broken in the crash.
   b) The department store stocks lots of babies' clothes.
   c) Our country's athletes always do well.
   d) The horses' manes were well groomed.
   e) The teachers' meeting took place after school.
   f) We could not see the ship's flag.

Practise your punctuation

1. Shanaz and Ali, who were playing in the park, pulled a thorn out of the dog's paw.
2. Charles Dickens, a famous author, wrote a book called Oliver Twist, in which Oliver became one of Fagin's thieves.
3. Dawn's early light crept into the cave's entrance, allowing the explorers to see the paintings on the wall.
4. My father's job, selling shoes, takes him all over England.
5. "I'm going to take a photograph of the dinosaurs' skeletons," said the professor.

Book 4

Unit 17 Standard English

Focus
Introducing the concept of Standard English

Definitions of terms used
Standard English is the kind of language we use in writing. It is used in education, government and business, and in most books.

Non-standard English is often used in everyday speech. We may say things differently from the way in which we would write them. Non-standard English may differ from Standard English in two ways:
- grammar (the way we form sentences)
- vocabulary (the words we use)

Teacher's notes
Standard English is the yardstick against which written English is assessed to test its grammatical correctness. (See the notes on page 4 for further information.)

Answers

Practice
1. Did you see that man with purple hair?
2. The old lady has a lot of cats.
3. Keep quiet and do not talk nonsense.
4. She's always eating. She is very greedy.
5. Shall we play truant from school today?
6. I spent five pounds on the chocolates.
7. That is very good.
8. Tell me where you hid the money.
9. I think Chelsea are excellent!
10. I will have sausages and mashed potatoes for dinner, please.

Making sure
1. Darren and I watched television.
2. Who has my pen?
3. They are coming soon.
4. He does not know anything.
5. I have not got any.
6. We were just looking.
7. I do not want any trouble.
8. What do you want?
9. I am going to get you.
10. That is the picture that I drew.

Practise your punctuation
1. Carlo opened the door, looking very grubby and dirty. Mrs Roberts, his mum, looked at him open-mouthed. "Just look at the state you're in. What you been up to?" "Well, me and Ruth was climbing the wall when I fell off of it," replied Carlo. "I ran home quick to tell you." Mrs Roberts looked at Carlo. "You think I'm gonna believe that? Go and wash, and get changed," she ordered. "It's not fair!" Carlo muttered. "I ain't done nothing wrong. You're always picking on me."

2. Carlo opened the door, looking very grubby and dirty. Mrs Roberts, his mother, looked at him in surprise. "Just look at the state you are in. What have you been doing?" "Well, Ruth and I were climbing the wall when I fell off," replied Carlo. "I ran home quickly to tell you." Mrs Roberts looked at Carlo. "Do you think I am going to believe that? Go and wash, and get changed," she ordered. "It's not fair!' Carlo muttered. 'I have not done anything wrong. You are always criticising me."

Unit 18 Sentences (double negatives; subject and verb agreement)

Focus
Double negatives; subject and verb agreement

Definitions of terms used
Two common grammatical mistakes are:
- writing sentences which contain double negatives
- writing sentences in which the subject and the verb do not agree.

A negative is a word, or part of a word, that means 'no'.

If the subject of the sentence is plural, the verb must also be plural.

Teacher's notes
Both these grammatical mistakes commonly occur in non-standard English. Children will have come across the words **negative** and **positive** in Book 2, and in other areas of the curriculum such as Maths and Science.

Some common negative words are: **no**, **not**, **nothing**, **never**, **nowhere**, and the contraction **n't**.

The need for subject/verb agreement has been stressed throughout the course.

Answers

Practice
1. There is<u>n't</u> <u>no</u> point in going out because it's raining. There is no (isn't any) point in going out because it's raining.
2. The referee said that he did<u>n't</u> want <u>no</u> trouble. The referee said that he did not want any (wanted no) trouble.
3. The burglar claimed that he was<u>n't</u> <u>nowhere</u> near the house when it was burgled. The burglar claimed that he was nowhere (was not anywhere) near the house when it was burgled.
4. I do<u>n't</u> belong to <u>no</u> swimming club. I do not belong to a swimming club.
5. The crocodile has<u>n't</u> got <u>no</u> whiskers. The crocodile has not got any (has no) whiskers.
6. The toy robot did<u>n't</u> do <u>nothing</u> when I wound it up. The toy robot did not do anything (did nothing) when I wound it up.
7. The witness said that she <u>never</u> saw <u>nobody</u>. The witness said that she saw nobody (did not see anybody).
8. Ranjit would <u>never</u> try <u>nothing</u> new. Ranjit would never try anything (try nothing) new.
9. We have<u>n't</u> got <u>no</u> bananas. We haven't got any (have no) bananas.
10. I <u>never</u> went <u>nowhere</u> yesterday. I did not go anywhere (went nowhere) yesterday.

Making sure
1. There were many feathers in his headdress.
2. Here are the winning Lottery numbers.
3. None of the dogs was hungry.
4. Emma isn't coming to art club today.
5. Does anyone know Tom's address?
6. Jamal did his work before he watched television.
7. It doesn't look a very nice day.
8. Every present was carefully wrapped.
9. Hannah and James weren't playing on the computer.
10. All children have to go to school.
11. Each of the children was telling the truth.
12. The teacher gave a spelling test.

75

Book 4

Practise your punctuation

Robert, who was smiling like a cat with the cheese, opened the door and shouted, "Mum, guess what! I did really well in the test at school today."

"That's nice," his mother replied. "What was the test you did?"

"It was a spelling test. Three of us who did well were allowed to go out to play early."

"It's a pity I haven't got any sweets, or I would have given you some for trying so hard," his mum said.

"My friend Jamie didn't get any right," Robert said, as he made himself a jam sandwich.

Unit 19   Nouns (gender)

Focus
The classification of nouns according to gender

Definitions of terms used
Nouns may be classified according to their gender. A noun may be masculine, feminine, common or neuter.

Teacher's notes
In English, the gender of a noun does not affect the article or the adjective ending, as it does in many languages.

An interesting development in recent years has been the decline of certain diminutive feminine nouns such as **actress** and **manageress**; the nouns **actor** and **manager** now tend to be used for both males and females.

Answers
Practice
1. boy – girl   father – mother   uncle – aunt
   son – daughter   nephew – niece   king – queen
   prince – princess   bridegroom – bride   man – woman
   husband – wife   brother – sister

2. a) My mother was talking to my aunt.
   b) The bride smiled at the woman who was taking the photographs.
   c) The queen was not pleased with her daughter, the princess.
   d) The eldest sister was going to be the queen.

Making sure
1. *Masculine*
   monk
   wizard
   bachelor
   earl

   Feminine
   nun
   policewoman
   grandmother
   stepmother

   Common
   pupil
   secretary
   doctor
   friend
   cousin

   Neuter
   tap
   hotel
   rocket

2. a) prince   m
   b) bride   f

   c) orphan   c
   d) racket   n
   e) author   c
   f) patient   c
   g) nephew   m
   h) dentist   c

Practise your punctuation

1-2 a) Hissing angrily, the snake (c) slithered towards the child (c).
   b) The Duke (m) and Duchess (f) of Windsor (n) attended the theatre (n) to see a play (n) by William Shakespeare (m).
   c) "What sort of soup (n) is this?" the old man (m) asked the restaurateur (c).
      "It's tomato soup (n), sir," she replied.
   d) The tongue-tied boy (m), who was blushing nervously, plucked up courage (n) to ask the girl (f) for a dance (n).
   e) The doctor (c) examined the patient (c) and said,
      'I think it's just a bad cold (n). You should be better in a few days (n).'

Unit 20   Shortening and Extending Sentences

Focus
Pronouns, adjectives, adverbs, phrases and clauses

Definitions of terms used
We can shorten sentences by changing nouns into pronouns.

We can extend sentences by adding adjectives, adverbs, phrases or clauses.

Teacher's notes
This unit revises work on the items of grammar listed above, and considers how sentences may be transformed by the addition or omission of them. This is an important aspect of refining a piece of writing.

Answers
Practice
1. a) The dog chased the boy. It chased him.
   b) The girl enjoyed swimming. She enjoyed it.
   c) The monkeys climbed the creepers. They climbed them.
   d) My friend and I ran to the shop. We ran to it.
   e) The prince mounted his stallion. He mounted it.
   f) The star telephoned her boyfriend. She telephoned him.

2. (open)

Making sure
1. a) Early in the morning, the tired, dusty camels crossed the hot, sandy desert.
   b) The hot air balloon, an enormous, gas-filled monstrosity, floated over the countryside.

Book 1

c) The spectators threw rotten tomatoes, very soft and squashy, at the actors.
d) The sun umbrella with red and white stripes blew into the sea.
e) The giant, a great tower of a man, strode towards the castle.
f) The owl went out hunting during the night.

2. (open)

Practise your punctuation

The strong easterly wind made the sails of the pirate ship billow. The ship, an old merchant galleon captured long ago, was sailing to the Caribbean.
"Look lively," snarled Carbuncle Cutlass, the captain, "or you'll feel the lick of my whip on your backs."
The crew, a ferocious band of cutthroats, struggled and sweated as they climbed the rigging, cursing the captain silently under their breaths.
"Land ahoy!" came the cry from the crow's nest. Everyone strained their eyes against the sun to see the faint outline of the mysterious island ahead.

Progress Test B

Answers

1. a) impatient
   b) invisible
   c) inexpensive
   d) imperfect
   e) impure
   f) insane
2. (open)
3. a) careful – care
   b) circular – circle
   c) woollen – wool
   d) friendly – friend
   e) beautiful – beauty
   f) golden – gold
   g) graceful – grace
   h) wintry – winter
   i) muscular – muscle
   j) cowardly – coward
4. a) The dog chased the postman because it thought he was a burglar.
   b) The greedy girl ate all the sweets before the others got home.
   c) After I had eaten my meal, I brushed my teeth.
   d) I opened the door when the bell rang.
   e) The old lady was still cold although the sun was shining.

5. a) because
   b) before
   c) after
   d) when
   e) although
6. a) I lost the bag which contained my packed lunch.
   b) My uncle, who is very rich, is buying a Rolls Royce.
   c) The toy yacht, which was made of wood, sailed down the river.
   d) The model, who looked very elegant, came down the catwalk.
7. a) People who really enjoy themselves are fun-loving.
   b) A man without a beard is clean-shaven.
   c) Someone who is good at gardening is green-fingered.
   d) Someone who is very tired may be sleepy-eyed.
   e) Most cats are smooth-coated.
8. a) the claws of a cat - the cat's claws
   b) the apron belonging to the chef - the chef's apron
   c) the car belonging to the thieves - the thieves' car
   d) the hats of the soldiers - the soldiers' hats
   e) the coat belonging to Mr Bristow - Mr Bristow's coat
   f) the headlights of the cars - the cars' headlights
9. a) The girl said, "I have not done anything wrong."
   b) Tom said he did not want any sweets.
   c) Mrs Cook did not see anyone she knew in town.
   d) I have not been anywhere near the wet paint.
   e) Neither Jane nor Marsha was late.
   f) My teacher gave me some homework yesterday.
   g) My father did the crossword easily.
   h) Each of the apples was round and red.
   i) The boys were fighting.
10. *Masculine*
    son
    husband
    Feminine
    aunt
    niece
    bride
    Common
    tourist
    bus conductor
    child
    Neuter
    paper
    lollipop
    cup
11. a) An adverb of time tells us when an action took place.
    b) An adjective phrase is a small group of words without a verb that tells us more about a noun.
    c) An abstract noun is the name of a thought, idea or feeling.
    d) A transitive verb is any verb that can take an object.
    e) A suffix is a group of letters we can add to the end of a word to change its meaning.
    f) A complex sentence contains at least one main clause and one or more subordinate clauses.
    g) Standard English is the form of English usually used in writing.
    h) The gender of a noun may be masculine, feminine, common or neuter.

Notes

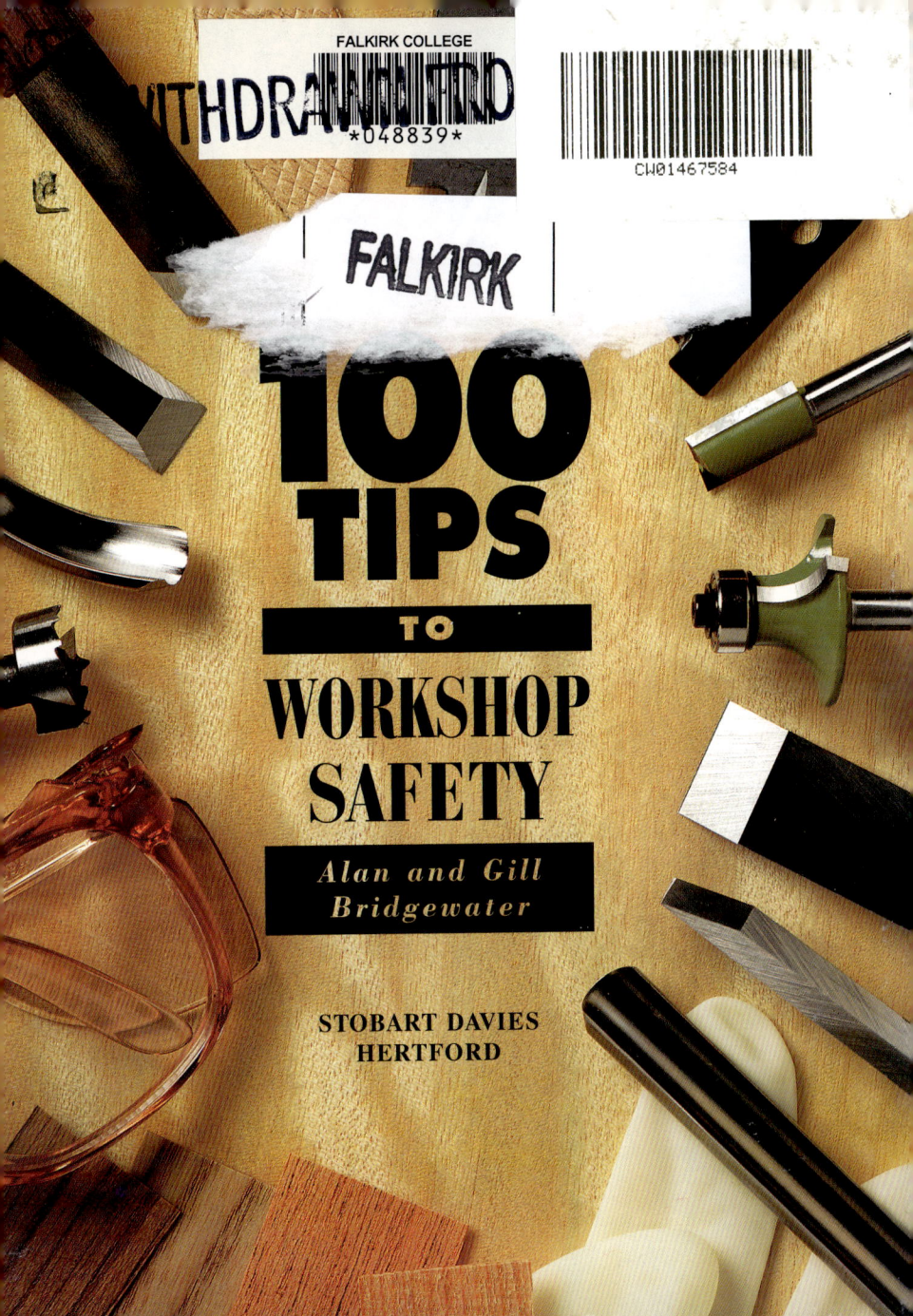

100 TIPS
TO
WORKSHOP SAFETY

Alan and Gill Bridgewater

**STOBART DAVIES
HERTFORD**

A QUARTO BOOK

Published in 1997 by
Stobart Davies Limited
Priory House
Priory Street
Hertford
Herts SG14 1RN

Copyright © 1996
Quarto Publishing plc.

All rights reserved. No part of this publication may be reproduced, stored in a retrieval system or transmitted in any form or by any means, electronic, mechanical, photocopying, recording or otherwise, without the permission of the copyright holder.

ISBN 0 85442 070 3

This book was designed and produced by Quarto Publishing plc
The Old Brewery
6 Blundell Street
London N7 9BH
Printed in China

Contents

INTRODUCTION
PAGE 6

SAFE WOODSHOP SETUP
PAGE 8

1 Floor Space *Page 8*

2 Wall Surfaces *Page 9*

3 Floor Surfaces *Page 10*

4 Anti-Slip Surfaces *Page 10*

5 Quiet Corner *Page 11*

6 Air and Windows *Page 11*

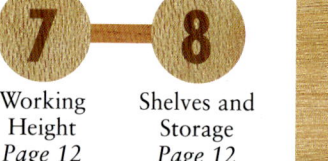

7 Working Height *Page 12*

8 Shelves and Storage *Page 12*

ELECTRICAL SAFETY
PAGE 13

9 Lighting *Page 13*

10 Wiring *Page 14*

11 Fluorescent Lighting *Page 15*

12 Circuit Breakers *Page 15*

13 Junction Box *Page 15*

14 Extension Cords *Page 15*

15 Outlets and Switches *Page 16*

16 Unplug for Safety *Page 16*

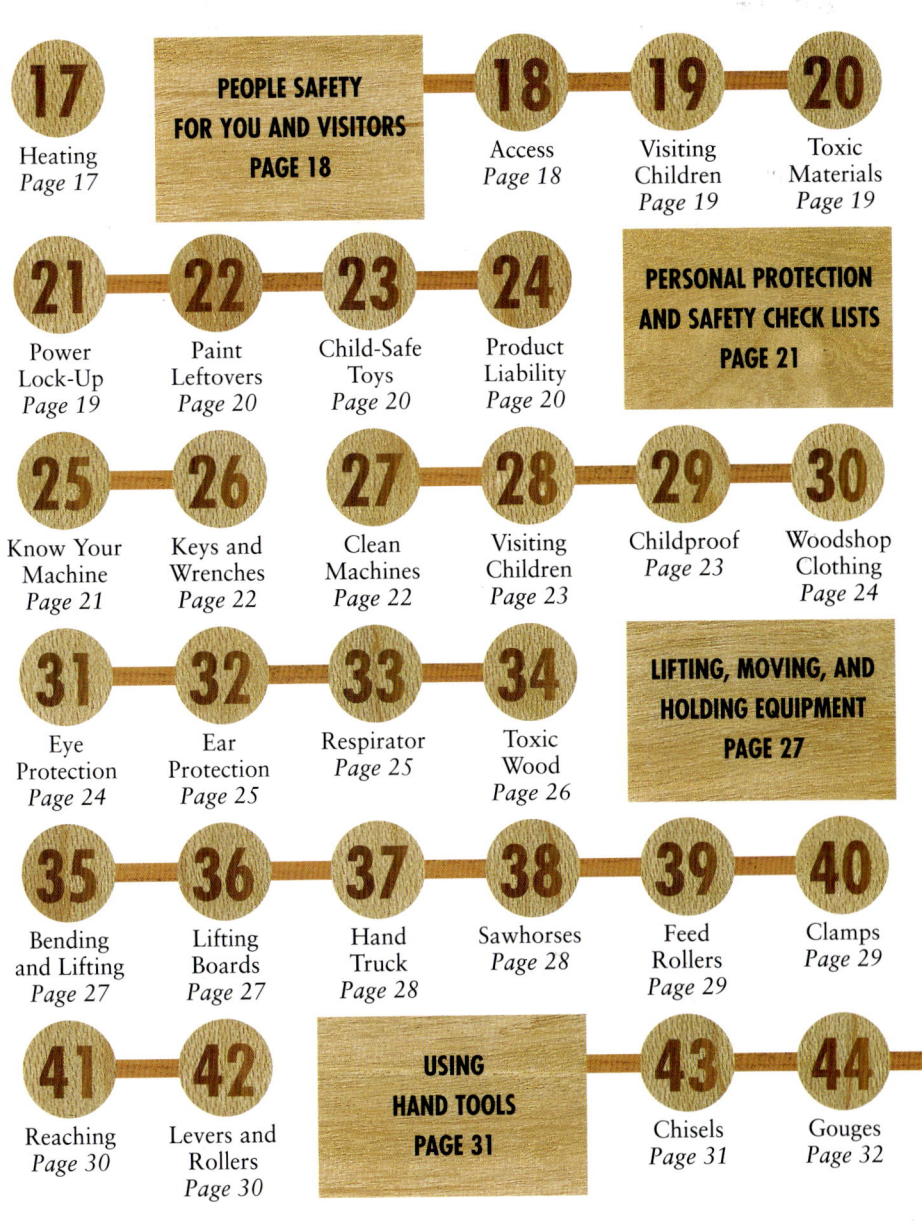

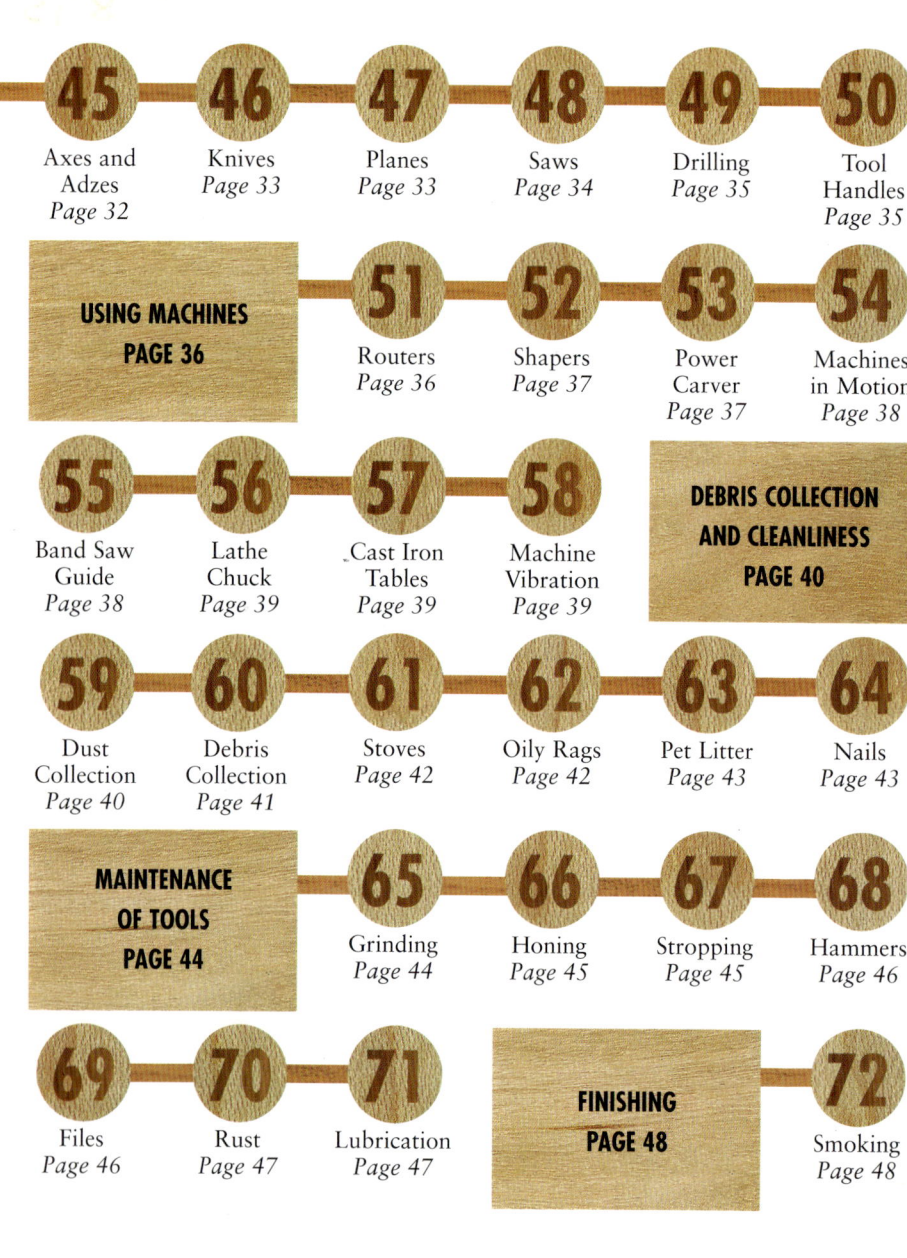

- **73** Sanding — *Page 48*
- **74** Allergic Reactions — *Page 49*
- **75** Finishes — *Page 50*
- **76** Painting Area — *Page 50*
- **77** Toxic Waste — *Page 51*

WHAT TO DO IN AN EMERGENCY — PAGE 52

- **78** Phone — *Page 52*
- **79** Work Programme — *Page 52*
- **80** Eye Injuries — *Page 53*
- **81** Cuts and Splinters — *Page 53*
- **82** First Aid Chart — *Page 54*
- **83** Fire Extinguishers — *Page 54*
- **84** Emergency Exits — *Page 55*
- **85** Smoke Alarms — *Page 55*
- **86** Severed Fingers — *Page 56*
- **87** Electrical Shock — *Page 56*
- **88** Severe Bleeding — *Page 56*

SPECIFIC MACHINE TOOL SAFETY — PAGE 57

- **89** Table Saw — *Page 57*
- **90** Portable Planer — *Page 58*
- **91** Band Saw — *Page 58*
- **92** Scroll Saw — *Page 59*
- **93** Router — *Page 60*
- **94** Lathe — *Page 60*
- **95** Plate Jointer — *Page 61*
- **96** Band Saw Blades — *Page 62*
- **97** Surface Planer — *Page 62*
- **98** Drill Press — *Page 63*
- **99** Machine Momentum — *Page 63*
- **100** Machine Location — *Page 63*

INTRODUCTION

SOMETIMES, IN THE COSY, quiet, dust-free corner of my workshop, at the end of the day when the sun's gone down, I take one of my pieces of woodwork, shut my eyes and run my finger tips over the joints and the textures. It's a great feeling to sit there, in my old armchair, to follow the knots and the grain, to relive the hours spent cutting the sap-sweet, butter-smooth wood, and then to open my eyes and wander around the workshop, and to know that the furniture, turnings, carvings and toys have been painstakingly worked with my own two hands. Woodworking is a uniquely creative experience that should not be missed. Okay, so we all know about the delights of woodworking, but what about the nightmare workshops, where the workers are dogged by cut and crushed fingers, sneezing and wheezing, strained muscles, and all the other horrors that haunt the craft. I'm sure you know what I mean – the workshops that are knee-deep in shavings, with frayed power cables snaking across the floor, and dust-laden cobwebs dripping from the ceiling, where the wheezing workers eat, drink and smoke amidst a morass of dust, debris, tools, noise and fumes. Yuck! Is it any wonder that such workshops are inefficient, with the stressed workers always bemoaning their bad luck!

Stop a moment and take a good long look at your hands. It's wonderful, isn't it – to think that your finger tips are so sensitive that they can feel degrees of texture too slight to be seen with the naked eye? Unfortunately, the grim and grisly reality of working in a sloppy, badly run workshop is that, before you can say choppers-whizzers-cutters-and-slashers, you can lose a finger, or damage your eyes or at the very least receive a nasty gash. Move your hands and ask yourself: Where would I be without those super-sensory digits?

In recent workshop safety surveys the real surprise is, not that woodworking tools are responsible for most hand-related industrial accidents, but rather that these same reports also declare that virtually all woodworking accidents could so easily be prevented. Still, the nightmare continues.

But enough of the agony and ecstasy of woodworking. I make no excuse for the purple shock-horror imagery, because the good news is that most workshop problems can be corrected simply by changing routines and procedures and/or by rethinking the way your tools and machines are organized. For example, since most power tool and machine accidents result from repetition, fatigue, overconfidence and inexperience – or a combination of all four – all you really need to do is to be aware of the problems and risks and then follow-through with a self-help program. Many safety aids can be made and up and running in just a few minutes. Better yet, you don't have to spend a lot on sophisticated widgets; all you need to do – as my granddad used to say – is read some, learn some and act some.

So there you go. If you want to achieve an optimum workshop environment, and cut down on the hazards and health risks, and in the doing smooth out your workshop operation and generally maximise your woodworking efficiency and creativity, then just keep reading.

We show you how.

SAFE WORKSHOP SETUP

Woodworking – carving, turning, furniture making, toymaking and all the rest – is a wonderfully joyous and therapeutic activity, but only if the workshop is clean, well organised and, above all, safe. The following primary pointers will help you create a positive, healthy, user-friendly workshop environment.

1 FLOOR SPACE Machines must be located so that there is room to manoeuvre. There needs to be plenty of all-round space, so that the workpiece can be freely fed into the machine at one side and extracted at the other. The amount of space should relate to the size and type of work produced. For example, the space needed to make small toys will obviously be less than that needed to make furniture. As timber always comes in lengths, and as the procedures necessarily involve walking from one machine to another – and all manner of bending, stretching and lifting activities besides – it is best to aim for as much space as possible.

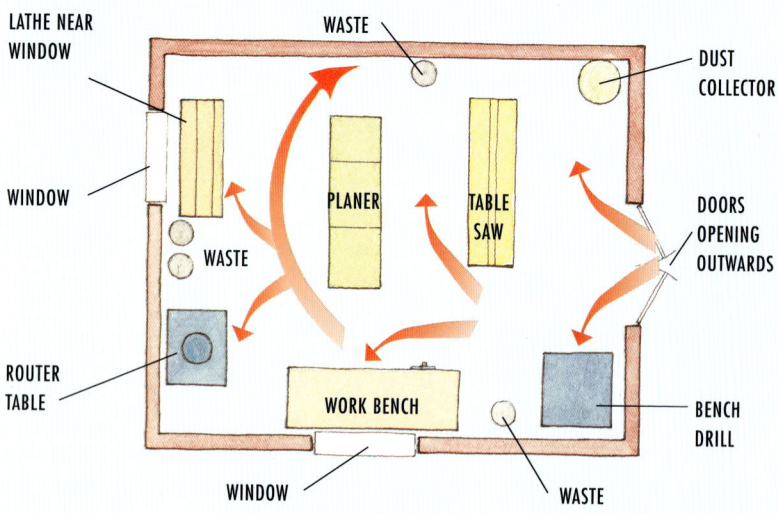

Arrange the worktables and machines so that you are able to move freely from one to another.

SAFE WORKSHOP SETUP

WALL SURFACES
Clean, bright walls make for a safe working environment. Though your workshop might well be built of anything from concrete block to wood framing, the actual interior wall surfaces need to be smooth, light in colour, fire resistant, dry and generally easy to clean and maintain. Most woodworkers favour white painted plasterboard or plywood for the walls and ceilings. Fibre or cork bulletin boards are useful for displaying designs, telephone numbers, timetables and the like; and battened areas are good for shelving. Some woodworkers find sections of pegboard useful for hanging up tools, but make sure peg hooks are secure so they don't come out when you pull down a tool.

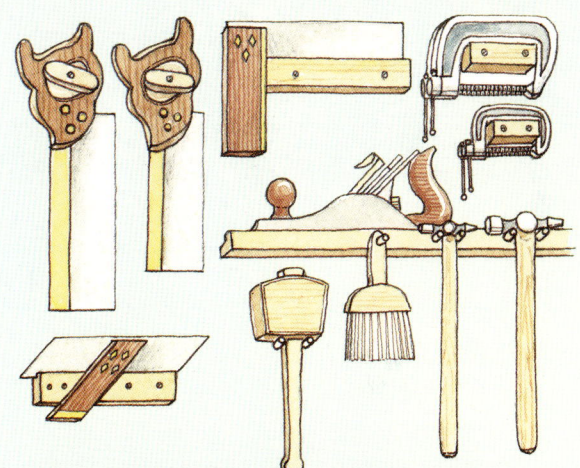

Organise your tool board with pegs and brackets so that everything is in full view and easy to reach.

Store all your heavy items on shelves and in pigeon holes.

SAFE WORKSHOP SETUP

Cushion-back vinyl

Untreated cork tile

Rubber tile

③ FLOOR SURFACES The floor surface should be stable, dry, hard wearing, fireproof, easy to clean, pleasing to the eye and non trip-and-slip. Most woodworkers favour a solid concrete slab, with selected areas covered with various secondary finishes. Depending upon your personal likes and needs – and of course the size of your bank balance – a concrete floor might be painted, or covered with industrial grade sheeting, rubber/cork/vinyl-tiled or even finished with strip hardwood. If you work for extended periods of time standing in one place, such as at a workbench or lathe, you may want to put down a rubber anti-fatigue mat.

BE WARNED – Steps, slight level changes, and slopes are a bad idea! – sooner or later you are going to trip over them. Worse still, such features, break up the useful floor area, restrict tool, machine and bench usage, and make sweeping and wet mopping even more of a chore.

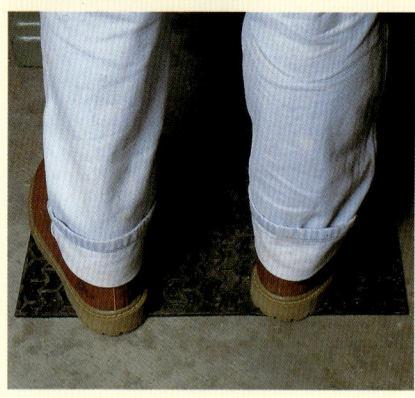

A rubber mat doubles up as an anti-fatigue surface and an anti-slip surface.

④ ANTI-SLIP SURFACES A considerable number of workshop accidents are caused by slippery floors. If you are at all worried about slipping – say in front of a hazardous machine like a lathe – you might consider creating anti-slip surfaces. A swift money-saver is to paint selected areas with a rubber type adhesive, sprinkle sharp, dry sand over the adhesive, wait for it to cure, and then sweep up the excess sand.

SAFE WORKSHOP SETUP

5 **QUIET CORNER** Knowing that fatigue is dangerous, it's a good idea to have a small area set aside for designing, contemplation and rest. If you like this notion, you could have the area carpeted and screened off from noise, dust and debris. Save money by fitting this area out with bits and pieces salvaged from your home – such items as a little table for drawing, a comfortable armchair and a cabinet for storing your drawing equipment. Don't forget the kettle!

6 **AIR AND WINDOWS** For health and safety's sake, clean air is a must. Your woodshop must be ventilated with opening windows and/or an air filter system. Planning regulations generally recommend that the area of opening windows must equal 20% of the total floor area. If you need to remove fumes and stale air, then you will require a positive-pressure ventilation system (**PPV**). A good, swift money-saver is to set a fan outside the workshop in such a way that fast-moving air tracks directly into the workshop and out through windows and vents. Or what better, on a summer's day, than to throw the doors open and work with plenty of sunshine and fresh air. In winter, you'll save on heating bills by keeping windows closed and using a ceiling-mounted recirculating air filter.

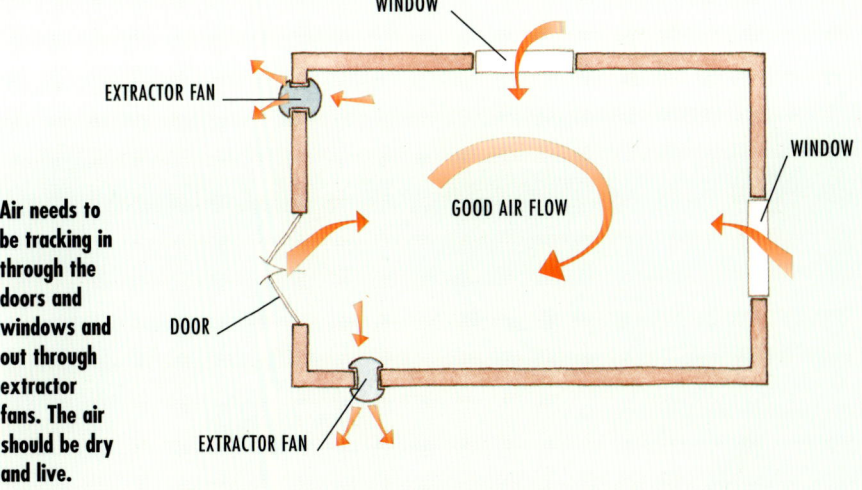

Air needs to be tracking in through the doors and windows and out through extractor fans. The air should be dry and live.

SAFE WORKSHOP SETUP

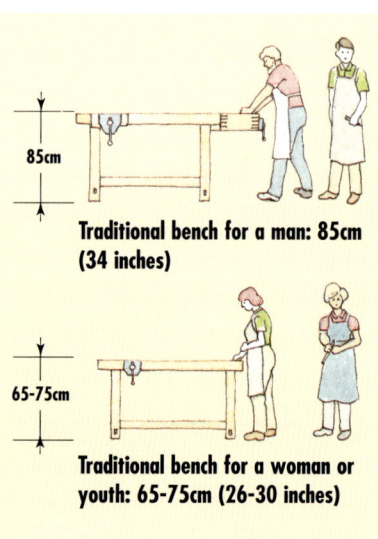

Traditional bench for a man: 85cm (34 inches)

Traditional bench for a woman or youth: 65-75cm (26-30 inches)

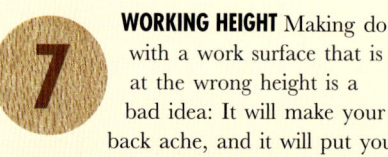

WORKING HEIGHT Making do with a work surface that is at the wrong height is a bad idea: It will make your back ache, and it will put you at risk when you either reach or stoop to work at a machine. A work surface – whether it is a work bench, desk or stand-up counter – must be at the correct working height. The height of a work surface should be adjusted to suit individual needs, but aim for a height that minimises stretch and shoulder hunch. The illustrated heights are a guide.

Stand-up counter: 80-85cm (32-34 inches)

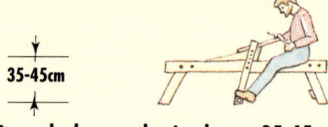

Sit-on donkey or shaving horse: 35-45cm (15-18 inches)

SHELVES AND STORAGE Safe and efficient workshops have one common feature: lots of well-planned storage – fixed shelves, freestanding units with movable shelving, built-in wall cabinets, under-bench shelves and cabinets and so on. If you stay with the following safe location pointers, you won't go far wrong:

- Site the shelves and cabinets so that they are easy to reach and so that you don't have to stretch over a machine.
- Make sure shelves don't overhang machines like lathes – you don't want a tool to slide off a shelf and onto a fast-spinning cutter blade or chuck.
- Make sure shelves are fixed to a stable surface so that they don't vibrate when the machines are powered up.

ELECTRICAL SAFETY

Though we are all familiar with electric lights and power outlets, it is this very familiarity that causes safety problems. The following guides and tips will enable you to run a safe and efficient woodshop. BE WARNED – With electricity, ignorance is more than dangerous – it is a potential killer! If you have any doubts about the following tips, or the condition and potential of your electrical system, then have it checked out by a qualified electrician.

9 LIGHTING Ideally, all machines and work surfaces need to be positioned so that there is a well-balanced mix of natural and artificial light. In windowless areas, take extra care to provide adequate lighting without shadows. Specific tasks, and left- and right-handedness might well call for additional lighting options. The overall goal is a lighting level that eliminates glare and hard shadow. For example, with a lathe positioned in front of a window, and with ceiling lights at top-centre, you might also require additional anglepoise lamps to your right, to throw light directly into the point-of-cut.

A badly lit lathe is dangerous.

Position a lamp for side light so that the working area is free from glare and shadow.

ELECTRICAL SAFETY

10 **WIRING** All electrical wiring must be in good condition and properly insulated. If the installation is old — say about 25-30 years — then it really needs replacing with modern insulated cable. It's best to check local building and electrical code requirements and have the system wired by a qualified electrician. Work with the electrician to locate wiring and outlets convenient to work areas with adequate provisions for both 240-volt and 415-volt circuits as needed. If your local code allows, you may want to consider locating cables in surface mounted channels. Then, not only can you swiftly and safely modify the system to meet your changing needs, but better yet, you won't have problems when you want to mount shelves and machines on the walls. You may also consider ceiling-mounted wiring for some machines.

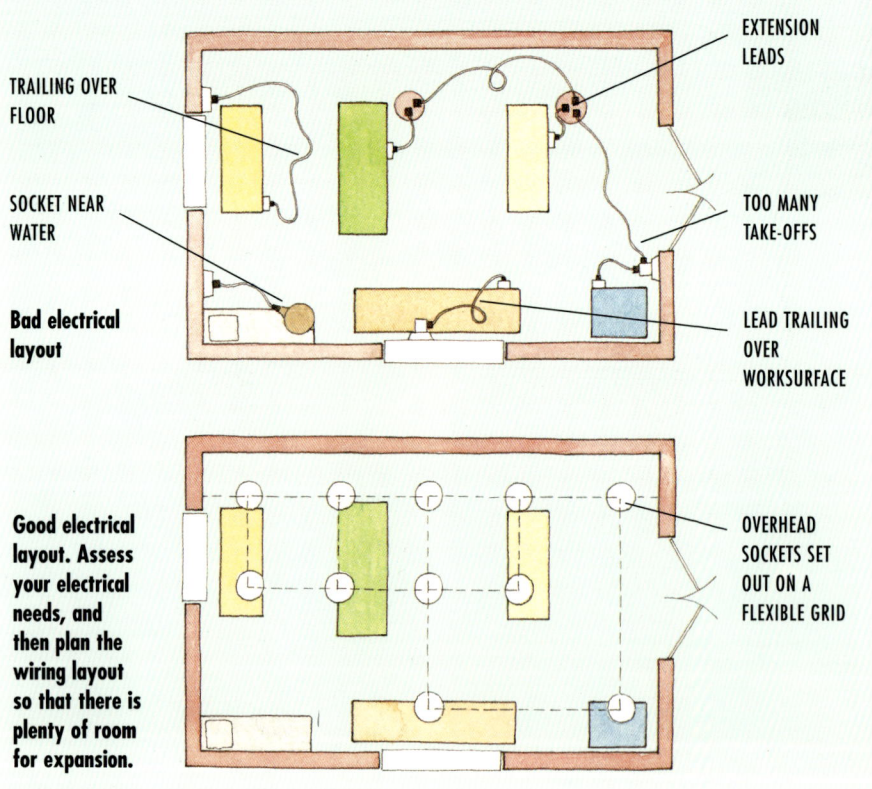

TRAILING OVER FLOOR

EXTENSION LEADS

SOCKET NEAR WATER

TOO MANY TAKE-OFFS

Bad electrical layout

LEAD TRAILING OVER WORKSURFACE

Good electrical layout. Assess your electrical needs, and then plan the wiring layout so that there is plenty of room for expansion.

OVERHEAD SOCKETS SET OUT ON A FLEXIBLE GRID

ELECTRICAL SAFETY

11 **FLUORESCENT LIGHTING** The most common and by far the most economical shop lights are fluorescent fixtures. They are many times more efficient than incandescent bulbs. They are also available in full-spectrum forms that simulate natural lighting. That's especially helpful for finishing where colour-matching is important. For those who complain that fluorescent flickering gives them headaches, non-flickering alternatives are also available, or you can stick with conventional lighting.

12 **CIRCUIT BREAKERS** You don't need to understand how circuit breakers work, but suffice it to say they are the primary way of protecting you and the machines from electrical damage. In use, the circuit breaker literally breaks the circuit when the system is overloaded, or when you do something stupid like banging a nail through a cable. Have your electrician make sure your circuit breakers and electrical service are adequate to your needs. Most homes typically have 100 to 200-amp electrical service. If you have an old system with fuses instead of circuit breakers, consider replacing it. Adding a residual current circuit breaker (RCCB) provides extra protection against short circuits and may be required by building codes in such installations as basements.

13 **JUNCTION BOX** The junction box houses the main switch and the circuit breakers or fuses for the whole electrical installation. As the unit is usually the first port of call when the power fails, or when there is a machine emergency, it follows that it needs to be located within easy reach. If your present unit is high up on the wall, in a dark cupboard or even outside, then consider having it relocated by a competent electrician.

14 **EXTENSION LEADS** In the context of workshop safety, extension leads are always a bad idea! If they are snaking across the floor or over work surfaces, then sooner or later you are going to trip over them, and/or damage them with a sharp tool or a heavy piece of equipment. Furthermore, longer leads steal power from electric motors and may result in premature motor failure. If you have no choice but to use an extension lead, be sure to have a portable circuit breaker in-line. Use the shortest cable and the largest wire gauge available to minimise voltage drop.

ELECTRICAL SAFETY

OUTLETS AND SWITCHES Isn't it always the case that power points seem to be on the wrong side of the room! If you are at the planning stage, then go for as many points as possible – one every four to six feet along walls is not outrageous. It's a good super-safe idea to have an emergency punch button or trip wire switch with every machine. Fit pull-cord switches near sinks and over benches. Many woodworkers eliminate the where-to-have-the-cable problem, by having the switches and sockets organized so that they are suspended from the ceiling. Floor-mounted outlets also work well for stationary machines.

The plug-still-in scenario is an accident just waiting to happen!

For optimum safety, pull out the plug and keep it in full view.

UNPLUG FOR SAFETY One of the most common causes of accidents is not taking the little extra time to do something the safe way. This is particularly true when it comes to electricity and machine set-ups. When it is time to change a bit or a blade, unplug the machine first. Don't take a chance on it accidentally getting switched on with your hand in the works. The best method whenever working on a machine is not only to unplug it, but to keep the cable end in plain view, so you know it's unplugged.

ELECTRICAL SAFETY

17 **HEATING** Cold fingers and toes equal slow response times; your workshop needs adequate heating. Oil-fired, electric and wood heat systems similar to those used in homes are all workshop options. Bear in mind that, whatever system you use, the object of the heating is two-fold – to keep you warm and to eliminate the condensation that does so much damage to tools and machines. If you must use temporary space heaters, always avoid gas and paraffin heaters that give off water vapour and also present a potential carbon monoxide hazard in a closed shop.

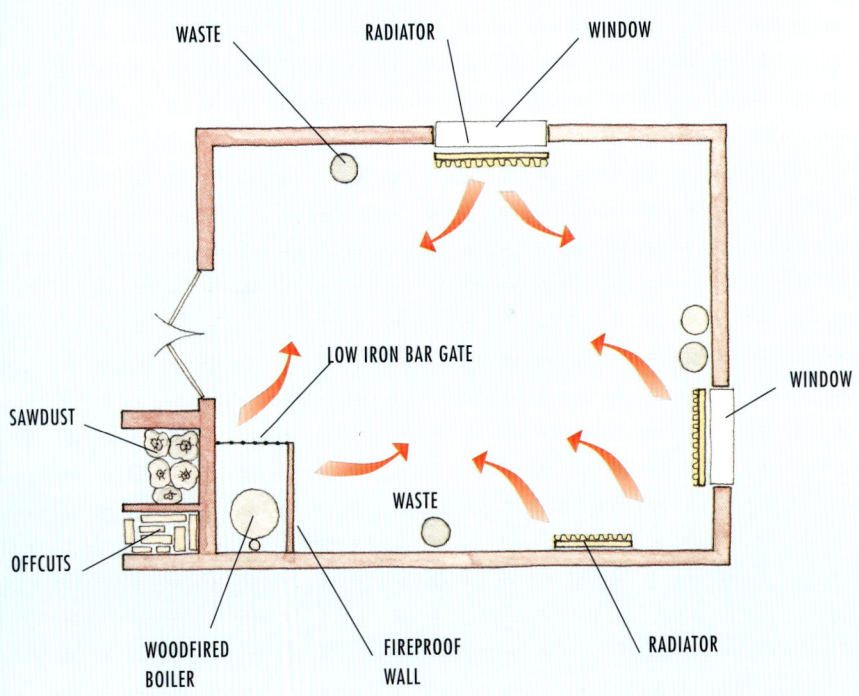

A ground floor workshop. An enclosed woodburning stove with a boiler and radiators is an all-round winner – it gets rid of your waste and keeps you warm. Plan the layout so that there is an adequate fuel storage area.

PEOPLE SAFETY – FOR YOU AND VISITORS

Of course, you may know how to look after yourself in a workshop, but what about visitors? Workshops are by their very nature both dynamic and dangerous, presenting extra hazards for children, pets, family and curious friends. That's all the more reason why the workshop environment needs to be clean, safe, tidy and secure. If your shop is safer for visitors, it will be safer for you.

18 ACCESS

Although all the doors and windows need to have locks and catches, on no account should you ever be locked in, or, say, the kids and family locked out. If you want to work without interruption, then put a notice outside the door. If you have a choice (check your local building regulations), make sure that all the doors open outwards and are fitted with catches that allow you to push your way out in case of an emergency. Ideally you need two doors, so that there is always at least one clear and convenient exit.

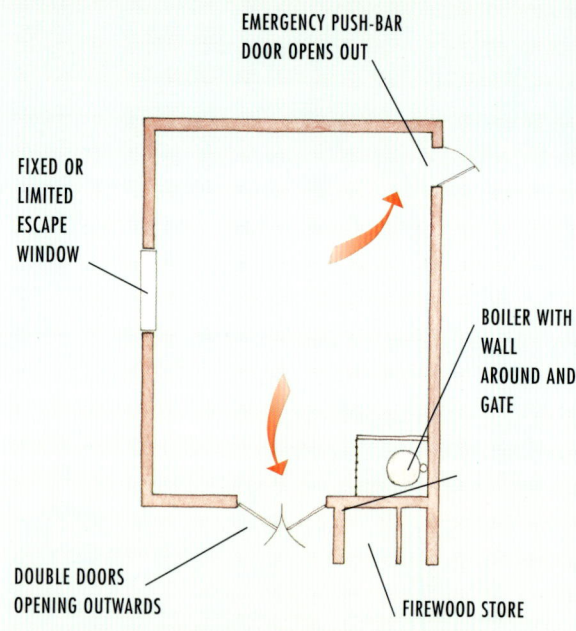

A ground floor workshop with minimum window openings. Every workshop needs two emergency exists – either two doors, or a door and an opening widow.

PEOPLE SAFETY - FOR YOU AND VISITORS

19 VISITING CHILDREN As most kids enjoy woodworking, it is important that they be encouraged to watch and participate, but do emphasise control and care. Allow no more than three at a time in the shop. Visiting kids should first be checked out to make sure that they are fitted correctly with appropriate clothing and safety equipment, such as safety glasses, hearing protection and a respirator if necessary. First sit them down at a safe watching distance, then show them on a hands-on basis how to perform a certain task. Keep sharp-edged tools as far back on the bench as possible, and the floor must not be cluttered with sharp-edged machinery. As kids are fascinated by machines and knives, always make sure that all doors and windows are locked when the workshop is not in use.

20 TOXIC MATERIALS Many workshop materials are inherently unsafe – some types of exotic wood, all wood dust, chemicals like acetone, methylene chloride, various paints, adhesives and varnishes, and so on. When you are using and storing products, be sure to read the manufacturer's guidelines, and then act accordingly. For most chemical products like paint and adhesives you can contact the manufacturer to obtain the Material Safety and Data Sheets (MSDS) that explain proper use and hazards. Some woods are toxic, so ask yourself before using a new wood: Is it used locally? Is it a traditional choice for the task you have in mind? If in doubt, seek the advice of a specialist supplier.

21 POWER LOCK-UP Many modern woodworking machines – lathes, band saws and the like – are fitted with a lock and/or have a removable on/off switch. The idea is that you can disable the machine when you are absent from the workshop.

Disable the machine by fitting a lock.

PEOPLE SAFETY - FOR YOU AND VISITORS

22 **PAINT LEFTOVERS** Yes, your grandpa's old leftover paint might still be in good condition, and yes, it will give a wonderfully glossy, hard-wearing finish, but of course, it will almost certainly contain highly poisonous lead! And many old powder pigments contain such delights as arsenic and antimony – both poisonous! On the premise that many old products are either toxic or corrosive – or both – the best advice is to dispose of them properly. Check with local officials about legal disposal of small quantities of hazardous waste.

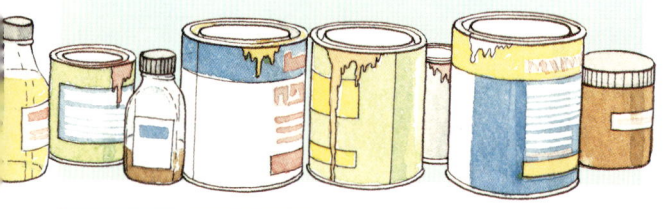

23 **CHILD-SAFE TOYS** Traditional wooden toys are great fun! – woodworkers like making them, and kids like playing with them. That said, you do have to bear in mind that finger-sticky toddlers are almost certainly going to be licking and sucking the toy, and generally doing their best to push it up their noses and in their ears – if not worse! You MUST make sure that the wood is splinter free, non-toxic and otherwise safe. Children's toys and furniture should conform to Toy Safety standards.

24 **PRODUCT LIABILITY**
If you have it in mind to sell your work – toys, furniture, turned bowls or whatever – then you are legally obliged to ensure the work is safe, and fitting the purpose for which it was designed. For example, if you make a bedside lamp for sale, then it is your responsibility to make sure that everything about the lamp is safe – the finish, the structure, the wood type and the electrical fittings. If you have doubts, contact local consumer groups and advisory bodies.

BE WARNED – Ignorance is no excuse!

PERSONAL PROTECTION AND SAFETY CHECK LISTS

With the increased use of woodworking machinery, it is becoming more and more important that woodworkers follow a programme of positive safety. You need to run through a general safety check before you switch on machines, and you need to wear suitable protective clothing. The following guides will help you to keep your body out of harm's way.

25 KNOW YOUR MACHINE

Having first read the owner's manual and made yourself familiar with the machine's function, you must always run through a pre-power check list. Ask yourself such questions as: Are the guards down? Does the on/off switch work? Are the tools out of harm's way? and so on. Being mindful that familiarity leads to all manner of potentially dangerous short-cuts, you should pin the check list up on the wall near the machine.

Lower the guard for optimum clearance.

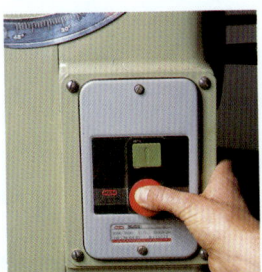
Always test switches before getting down to work.

Adjust the band saw guard so that there is about 1cm (½ inch) clearance.

Set the drill press guard so that the chuck is covered but still in clear view.

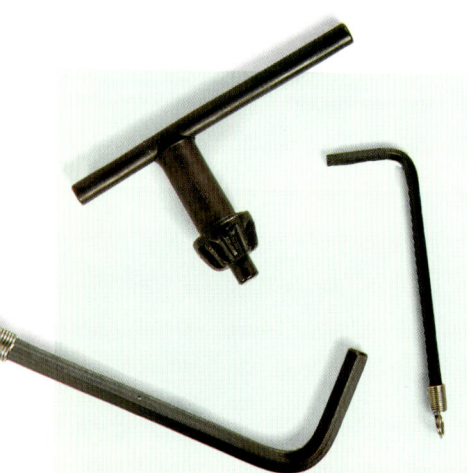

KEYS AND WRENCHES Before you switch on, make sure that you have removed chuck keys and Allen wrenches. This is particularly important in the context of lathe and drill press chuck keys. If you can't remember to remove the key before switch-on, then make a huge ring for the key out of plywood or coloured wire – so big that it's an unavoidable hindrance – or simply chain the key to the machine base.

CLEAN MACHINES Keep the area in and around the machine clean and uncluttered. Dust, oil and debris invite accidents. Wood shavings are particularly dangerous as they gradually polish the floor to a shiny finish.

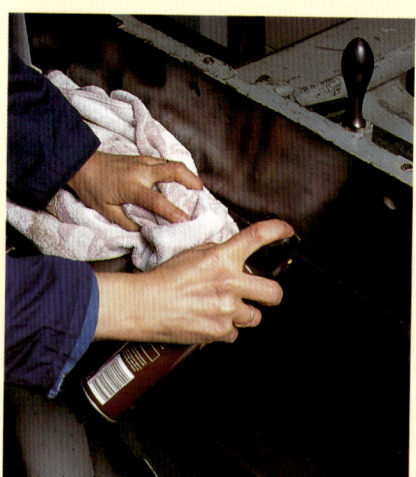

Polish the work bed to reduce potentially dangerous friction.

Clean up the dust and debris as soon as the job is complete.

PERSONAL PROTECTION AND SAFETY CHECK LISTS

Never leave the key in the lathe chuck.

28 VISITING CHILDREN Always welcome your children in the workshop, but provide them with safety goggles, and sit them down at a safe distance. Use this quality time to educate the kids in the safe use of the machines. Bear in mind – before switching on portable planers, etc – that the waste wood is invariably spat out at child's-eye level.

Use a small brush to clean out the 'stop' and 'guard' channels.

29 CHILDPROOF Children are always curious, so be sure to lock up the workshop, and remove start-up keys. If you have a home workshop and kids, then you must follow a programme of positive education and protection. If your kids are at the got-to-give-it-a-try stage, then fit padlocks to all the machines.

23

PERSONAL PROTECTION AND SAFETY CHECK LISTS

30 **WORKSHOP CLOTHING** Many accidents have to do with clothing, etc. getting dragged into the machines. Make sure that you are dressed appropriately for the job – no loose hair, dangling neckties, or jewellery, no flapping cuffs or loose clothes. A guide and simple solution is to wear a hat, and to have a workshop coat with button-up cuffs.

Safety glasses

Safety goggles

31 **EYE PROTECTION** Workshops are inherently dangerous – fast-spinning machines, fragments of wood flying through the air, tools and machines that have the potential to fail catastrophically, and all the rest. You must wear protective glasses or a full-face mask. Don't think you can cut costs by using items like swimming goggles, because they can shatter into sharp-edged splinters. Get yourself a pair of approved safety glasses – and use them!

PERSONAL PROTECTION AND SAFETY CHECK LISTS

32 EAR PROTECTION High speed woodworking machines can be incredibly noisy. For example, some portable planers are so noisy that five minutes running time will leave your ears ringing and you feeling generally numbed and confused. It follows that you need to be wearing ear protection. To make ear protection even safer you should get a flashing light for the phone and work out hand signals so you can communicate with your workshop mate.

Ear defenders

33 RESPIRATOR The fine wood dust created by high speed machines is a hazard. The dust can result in breathing problems, skin rashes, dry eyes and all manner of health and safety delights. Dust is even more of a problem if you have it in mind to work with exotic tropical wood. Many woodworkers now wear helmet-mask type respirators. In use, the self-contained unit sucks air up through a filter and plays it down over your face to create a positive air environment. Yes, these respirators are expensive, but then again, they double as eye protectors and some even offer ear protection. They can be worn over spectacles, long hair and whiskers.

Full face mask and respirator

25

PERSONAL PROTECTION AND SAFETY CHECK LISTS

Iroko ✗

Afrormosia ✗

Jelutong ✗

European walnut ✓

American red elm ✓

American red oak ✓

34 **TOXIC WOOD** Some woods are toxic – to the touch, to breathe in as dust, when they are in contact with some foods, when they are in contact with eye and nose membranes, and so on. If you are anxious about the notion, then the best safeguard is to follow approved health and safety recommendations as already described, and then have a policy of only using traditional tried and tested varieties.

LIFTING, MOVING AND HOLDING EQUIPMENT

Maybe you are strong enough to lift and heave just about anything and everything that your workshop is going to throw at you, but what's the point? Workshop skills are not about gut-heaving feats of strength. Rather they have to do with being able to perform all the tasks skilfully and efficiently with the minimum of sweat and tears. The following tips will show you the best way forward.

BENDING AND LIFTING
When you come to lift a heavy chunk of wood like a big turning blank or a small log from floor level, squat down, with your knees together, throw your arms around its middle – as if you were cuddling your mum – and then straighten your legs nice and easy.

BE WARNED – if you stoop over a heavy item, and try to lift it with a loose, belly-sagging, knees-apart, curved-back action, then you are asking for problems. If your work requires lots of lifting or bending, consider wearing a back support belt for extra protection against injury.

LIFTING BOARDS When you are lifting heavy man-made boards up from the floor to the bench – say a 5mm (¼-inch) thick sheet of plywood, chipboard or MDF – you most certainly put yourself at risk if you try to do it on your own. If you are a one-man band – or even a one-woman band – strap it with a flat webbing to make a handle, stand in a well-braced upright position, and use a controlled lift-and-slide action to ease it up onto the bench.

Adjust the straps so that the point of lift is at a comfortable height.

LIFTING, MOVING AND HOLDING EQUIPMENT

HAND TROLLEY A small combination dolly or hand trolley is a wonderfully efficient low-cost piece of safe-to-use equipment – perfect for moving small heavy items like bits of machinery and various logs and short lengths of timber. A good money-saver is to go for one of the old-fashioned wood and steel-type trolleys that were traditionally used for moving very heavy weights like beer barrels and bags of sand. These can often be purchased second-hand.

A flatbed trolley enables you to move heavy loads with the minimum of effort.

SAWHORSES Fold-up sawhorses are primarily used for supporting materials that are too large for your bench. You could manage with a couple of old wooden crates or an upright chair, but a folding sawhorse is manageable and easy to store. Save money and make your own. Aim for a closed-up height of about 90cm (36 inches).

A matched pair of sawhorses makes for a safe sawing set-up.

Trestles and sawhorses are invaluable around the workshop.

LIFTING, MOVING AND HOLDING EQUIPMENT

39 **FEED ROLLERS** If you repeatedly need another pair of hands to help you support and guide stock into a machine or across a bench, then maybe you ought to consider getting yourself a pair of feed rollers. In use, the rollers are mounted on stands at the height of the work surface, and then simply located in line so that the stock is supported – like a conveyor belt. Feed rollers are a great way of reducing the risk of machine kick-back and/or jamming – when the sagging workpiece goes out of control. Feed rollers come in two types: One is a typical cylindrical roller, the other is made up of a line of rolling balls. The ball-type has the advantage of letting stock move in any direction across its surface.

Roller stand

40 **CLAMPS** Generally speaking, woodworkers need a lot of clamps – G-clamps, pipe clamps, sash clamps and all the rest. Save money by buying only the sizes and types to suit the job at hand, then you won't be wasting your cash on a clamp that's never going to be used. Being mindful that G-clamps are sometimes used in potentially dangerous situations, only buy clamps that are forged.
BE WARNED – Cheap cast iron clamps are a bad idea, because they can fail catastrophically – with lots of sharp edges, and with the workpiece springing back out of control.

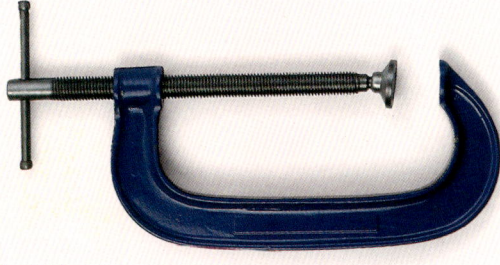

Quality G-Clamp

LIFTING, MOVING AND HOLDING EQUIPMENT

41 REACHING It doesn't matter how tall or short you are: If you are stretching and reaching, then you are doing it wrong. Not only is there the potential for falling or damaging your back, but if machines are involved, the hazards increase. Stretching to control a workpiece on a table saw, for example, could very quickly bring you in contact with the saw blade. If you repeatedly find yourself stretching or reaching, then ask yourself why. Is the shelf too high? Is the bench too wide? Is the walk-around space restricted? Then solve the problem by getting a pair of steps, or lowering the shelf, or whatever seems appropriate.

42 LEVERS AND ROLLERS Who ever said, 'Give me a lever long enough, and I will move the moon' – was it Archimedes? – certainly knew what he was talking about. If for example, you want to move a dead weight – you know, something like a table saw or lathe – from one side of the room to the other, then using wooden rollers and a length of timber for a lever is the safe, sure answer.
BE WARNED – never be tempted to use metal-on-metal – meaning a metal bar to lever a cast iron machine. If you do, you risk fracturing the iron.

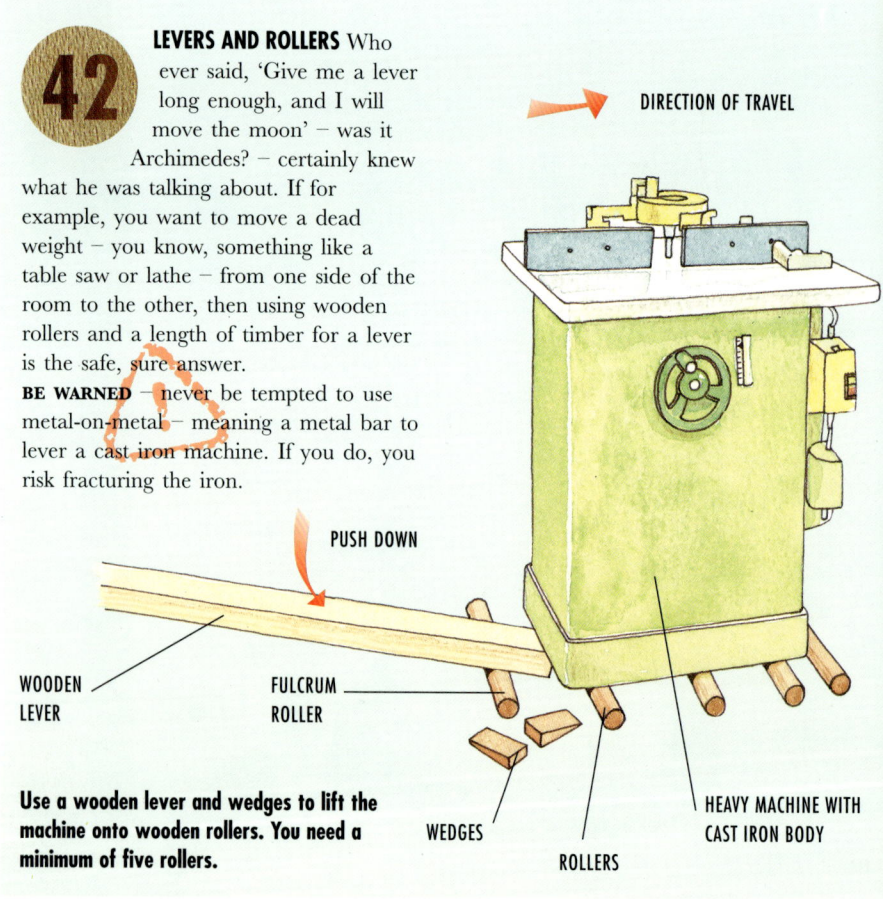

DIRECTION OF TRAVEL

PUSH DOWN

WOODEN LEVER

FULCRUM ROLLER

WEDGES

ROLLERS

HEAVY MACHINE WITH CAST IRON BODY

Use a wooden lever and wedges to lift the machine onto wooden rollers. You need a minimum of five rollers.

USING HAND TOOLS

Woodworking, whether it be carpentry, woodturning, carving or whatever, is to a great extent a simple matter of cutting and shaping wood with traditional sharp-edge hand tools. Tools like the saw, adze, axe, plane, chisel, gouge and knife are all basic to woodworking. So it logically follows that a good part of workshop safety has to do with being able to use such edge tools with the minimum of effort. The following pointers will show you how to use and care for the primary cutting tools.

43 CHISELS Of all your hand tools, the chisels are, at one and the same time, the most widely used, the most open to abuse and the most vulnerable. If you have a choice and are buying new, go for hand-forged laminated steel blades, with fully honed ready-to-use cutting edges. The laminated steel will hold an edge longer. The guards that are usually supplied with the tools are designed to protect both you and the cutting edges – so don't lose them. Store chisels at a low level – never high up on a shelf where they are hard to reach and might fall, potentially damaging both you and their fine cutting edges.

Work with a safe two-handled cut – one hand pushing and the other holding and guiding.

When the job is done, protect the razor-sharp bevel edge with a plastic guard.

USING HAND TOOLS

44 GOUGES Carving is currently one of the fast growing woodcrafts, so even if you don't carve now, you will most likely eventually purchase and use one or more gouges. If you are a raw beginner and worried about safety, you won't go far wrong if you stay with these three rules of thumb:
- Always have the workpiece well supported with a clamp or bench holdfast.
- Always use a braced two-handed grip.
- Always cut away from your body.

1. Secure the workpiece with a clamp or bench stop.

2. Hold the tool with two hands and work at a low skimming angle. Use the guiding hand to fine-tune the cut.

45 AXES AND ADZES
Axes and adzes are commonly perceived as being not only anachronisms in a modern workshop, but difficult and dangerous tools to use. But if they are used with care and caution, they are both efficient and safe. Be mindful that the working height is critical, and the pendulum action is such, that it's not easy to stop the motion once the swing is under way. Set yourself up with a selection of log-section cutting blocks – so that you can always choose a safe working height to suit the task in hand.

BE WARNED – As older kids like the notion of axes and adzes, first show them how they are correctly used. This diminishes the forbidden-naughty-but-nice dynamics that some kids get into. Then be sure to store the tools under lock and key.

USING HAND TOOLS

46 **KNIVES** The knife is often taken for granted, but one look over the average workshop will confirm that it is still a primary tool. In use – mostly in carving – knives are wonderfully safe, as long as they are manoeuvred, either with a braced two-handed away-from-the-body cut, or with a single-handed thumb-braced apple-paring cut. And, don't forget, a sharp knife is much safer to use than a blunt one that has to be forced through the work.

The levering action controls the cut.

47 **PLANES** Although portable power planers are showing up in more workshops, hand planes are still the first-choice tool for making wood straight, flat, square and smooth. It's amazing how many woodworkers have plane-related accidents – damage to the workpiece, bloody knuckles, or bruised toes. First and foremost, the workpiece must be held securely, either in the vice, or with a hold-down. Secondly, in use, you need to make sure that the hand holding the body of the plane is positioned so that you don't get splinters or friction burns. Lastly, as planes are both heavy and relatively fragile, keep them away from the edge of the bench. A bruised toe and a cracked plane – what a mistake!

Secure the workpiece in the vice.

Make sure that your hands are in control and out of harm's way.

USING HAND TOOLS

48 **SAWS** Most hand-saw accidents have to do with bad storage, or with blade slipping when the cut is being initiated. The first problem is easily solved: All you do is cover the teeth with a guard – a plastic strip or a wrap of old cloth – and be sure to store the saw where it can be seen and effortlessly reached. To avoid blade slipping, the safest procedure for starting a cut is to make a series of small dragging strokes until the teeth have made their mark. Rusty, blunt saws invariably jump and slip. Thus it follows that you won't go far wrong on the safety front if you always keep the blade sharp and rust free.

Handsaw

Do not use the tip of your thumb to guide the saw blade.

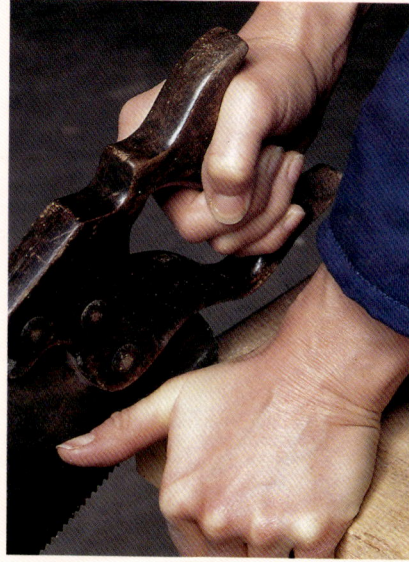

Use the heel of your thumb to steady the blade.

USING HAND TOOLS

49 **DRILLING** Most drilling accidents have to do with the workpiece spinning off out of control to do damage to itself and anything that happens to be in its trajectory. Avoid such mishaps by being sure to clamp the workpiece down whenever possible. For clean, flat-bottom holes in wood, use Forstner type bits.

50 **TOOL HANDLES** A badly designed or broken tool handle inevitably results in a poor grip, and a poor grip causes friction and fatigue damage to your hands. All of that adds up to an accident in the making. Always make a point of ensuring that all handles – especially axes, adzes, chisels and gouges – are comfortable to hold and well fixed.

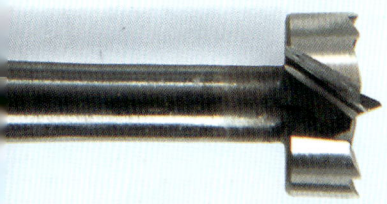

When using Forstner drill bits, a build-up of shavings in the hole can cause the bit to jam in the workpiece. For best results, use a slow drill speed and more than one plunge.

Flat bits must be used at high speed to minimise wander and chatter. Avoid using bits with bent shanks as the vibration will dislodge the workpiece.

Damaged tool handles

USING MACHINES

Modern woodworking machines are a joy – they are relatively inexpensive, easy-to-use, efficient and generally safe. That said, if accidents do occur, they can be extremely serious – even life threatening. You must keep your machines in peak condition; you must read the manuals supplied with the machines; and you must take reasonable care. The following tips will show you how.

51 ROUTERS Many router accidents relate to poor control. The router rotates at very high speeds – much faster than most power tools. A variable speed router allows you to hold back on the power until you are just about to make contact with the workpiece and then match the power to the job at hand. This procedure ensures that you are the master – not the tool! It's vital that you always feed your work in the correct direction – against rather than with the spin of the router bit. Otherwise the bit may slip and skate along the workpiece. Check with the manual and the cutter head type, and follow the recommendations for your machine.

A hand-held router needs to be used with care and caution.

Note the direction of spin in relationship to the direction of feed.

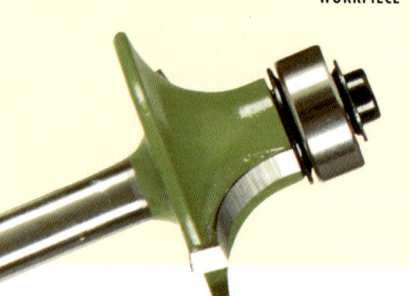

USING MACHINES

SHAPERS

52 The shaper is one of the most dangerous machines in your workshop simply because it's difficult to guard against the fast-spinning cutter. Your best line of positive defence is to familiarise yourself with the direction of spin – it might even be reversible – and then set up jigs and side tables, so that you can feed the workpiece with a steady strong hand and maximum control. Use of zero-clearance auxiliary fences, anti-kickback fingers and push sticks all add to safety.

Never work with the guard in the 'up' position.

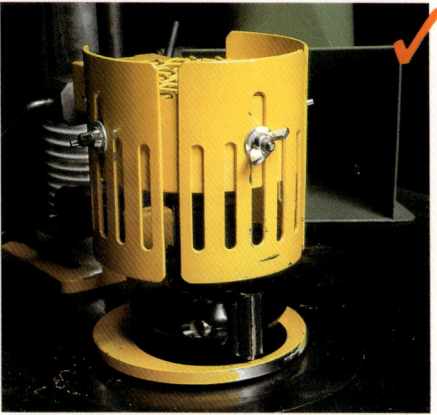

Adjust the guard height shields so that they fit the size of the workpiece.

53 POWER CARVER A power carver can be anything from a high-tech tool with a reciprocating gouge head or a sophisticated rotary tool that can carve in miniature, through to a large angle grinder or even a router-type option fitted onto a power drill. Regardless of the variations, the overall dangers have to do with dust, noise, and hand control. Always secure the workpiece in a vice or with a holdfast, and always wear goggles and a respirator. **BE WARNED** – a hot tool or shaft is an early warning that the bearings need re-greasing and/or the air feed is choked with dust.

USING MACHINES

54 MACHINES IN MOTION

Many accidents have to do with not appreciating that such-and-such a quiet-running machine is actually in motion. A low-cost solution is to apply a dash of color to wheels and other moving parts, so as to create a flicker-warning when the machine is in action.

55 BAND SAW GUIDE

The safety function of the band saw blade guide is two-fold – the lowered guard stops you from accidentally touching the blade, while at the same time the guides and bearings at the back of the guard help keep the blade in line and prevent catastrophic blade failure. Always lower the guard to permit just enough clearance of the workpiece under the guard. That will ensure maximum support for the blade as well as maximum safety for you.

1. Adjust the guide so that the back edge of the blade is supported.

2. Align the runners so that the blade is centralised.

3. Fine-tune the wheel-stop so that there is a slight clearance at the back edge of the blade.

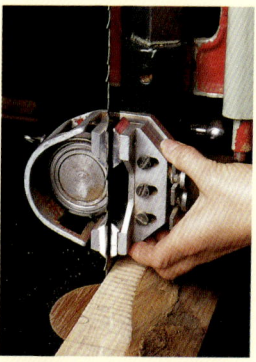

4. Adjust the height of the guide/guard so that it is about 1cm (½ inch) clear of the workpiece.

USING MACHINES

LATHE CHUCK Though a four-jaw chuck is one of the best ways of securing the workpiece, there is the danger that you will brush your left arm or hand up against the protruding jaws of the chuck while the lathe is in motion. An inexpensive guard can be made by bending a sheet of 3mm (⅛-inch) thick plywood in a curve, and fixing it in place with a couple of G-clamps – so that it bridges the chuck.

The easy-to-make guard protects your left arm from the spinning chuck.

CAST IRON TABLES If your machine table surfaces become so gummed up that they require a great deal of effort to keep the workpiece moving, then they are most certainly dangerous. The simplest safety action is to first clean off the resin with a fine emery cloth, then clean the surface with a spirit-soaked cloth, and finally polish the whole surface with one or other of the graphite anti-friction products that are on the market.

MACHINE VIBRATION If you find that one of your cast iron machine stands develops a potentially dangerous vibration, first check for loose parts or adjustments. If you find the cause is an uneven floor, the easiest and cheapest solution is to level it with a wedge. This is achieved by first cutting a hardwood wedge and a piece of 5mm (¼-inch) thick plywood. Smear glue over mating faces on the plywood and the wedge. Then tap them in place at the base. When the glue is set, use an old saw or chisel to cut the wood back flush with the machine.

DEBRIS COLLECTION AND CLEANLINESS

Wood dust not only harms the lungs, clogs the machines and is a fire risk, it also has the potential to creep from the shop environment back to home and hearth. As for all the offcuts, disposal is an ever-pressing chore. There is clearly a correlation between cleanliness and safety. The following tips will show you the way.

59 DUST COLLECTION According to International Safety Standards you should limit your exposure to fine wood dust. In very broad terms, they suggest that if you were to puff a heaped teaspoon of dust into the average garage-size workshop and then spend more than fifteen minutes a day in this atmosphere, you would be exceeding safe limits. For safety's sake, you need to stay with the following rules of thumb:
- Cut down on the amount of dust at source – by using filtered machines, and/or by producing shavings rather than dust.
- Capture as much dust as possible by using a vacuum system.
- Wear a dustmask/respirator.

Make sure that all your small power tools are fitted with dust bags.

Use a mobile dust vacuum system to service individual machines.

DEBRIS COLLECTION AND CLEANLINESS

Be mindful that tools are easily lost amidst floor shavings.

A build-up of debris can easily impede the safe running of a machine.

Be warned – a build-up of sawdust and machine oil is a dangerous mix!

60 DEBRIS COLLECTION

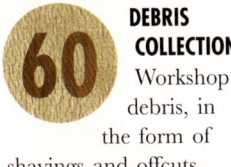

Workshop debris, in the form of shavings and offcuts scattered around on the floor, is a dangerous nuisance. On the one hand the shavings will polish the floor to the extent that it becomes slippery, and on the other hand, loose offcuts can easily be tripped over. It's good workshop practice to make a point of sorting the debris into stuff that can be used for small projects, bits that might be recycled into, say, dowels etc, and pieces that need to be thrown away.

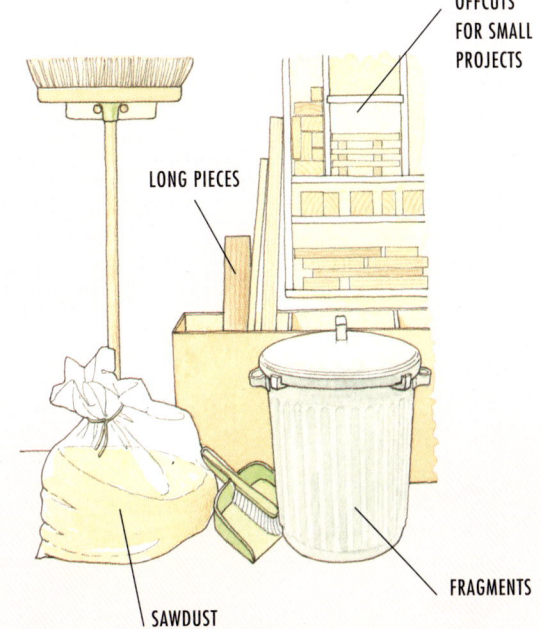

Organise your debris collection for maximum efficiency – bags for dust, rubbish bins for fragments, and racks and boxes for reusable offcuts.

DEBRIS COLLECTION AND CLEANLINESS

61 **STOVES** More and more, woodworkers are coming around to the idea, that perhaps the best user-friendly option for disposing of wood waste – dust and offcuts – is to burn it in a super-efficient woodburning stove. With the opportunity for a dry atmosphere for the tools, a clean floor AND warm fingers, nose and toes, a woodburner is a great money-saving idea. However, make sure that it is installed properly according to local fire and building regulations. Otherwise, your friendly woodstove may introduce a serious fire hazard to your workshop.

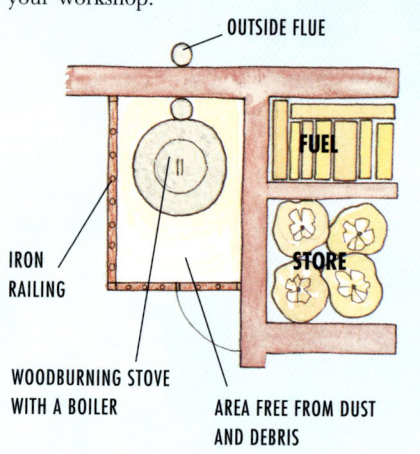

Fence the woodburning stove off behind a metal railing or cage.

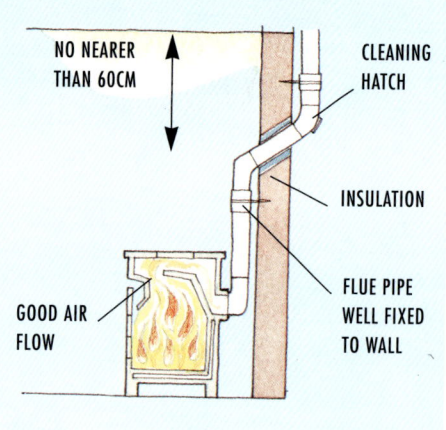

Be sure to follow installation safety codes.

62 **OILY RAGS** Oily rags – meaning rags soaked in motor oil, solvents, French polish, varnish, linseed oil, brush cleaner and such like – are dangerous. Under certain warm-and-enclosed conditions, the rags can smoulder and spontaneously combust. Remove the rags from your workshop as soon as you have finished with them. Damp them down and put them into a metal bin. On no account drop the rags into a plastic dustbin or seal them up in a plastic bag, as this can increase the risk of fume build-up and fire. Special air-tight metal cans are available for temporary rag disposal.

DEBRIS COLLECTION AND CLEANLINESS

63 **PET LITTER** If you do decide to use your shavings and wood dust as pet litter – say bedding for your rabbits, or a tray for your cat, or whatever – then you must remember, that the fine dust is just as harmful for your pets as it is for yourself.

64 **NAILS** A vast number of very painful workshop accidents have to do with woodworkers stepping on nails – meaning nails that have been hammered through a bit of wood, and then left around on the floor. The best defence is to remove the nail or scrap wood. If you are too busy, at least hammer the nail over so that it doesn't stick up.

1. Never leave nail-spiked offcuts sitting around on the floor.

2. Remove nails with a claw hammer and wear thick soled safety boots – just in case you miss a nail!

3. If you are short of time, then swiftly hammer the nails over and go back to them another day.

MAINTENANCE OF TOOLS

There is an old woodworking adage that asserts that a swift, sharp blade is a good deal safer than a slow, dull one. If you find that your cutting edges need to be forced into action, it is a sure indicator that you and the tools are at risk. The following tips will show you how to sharpen and care for your cutting edges, and in so doing make your workshop safer and more efficient.

65 GRINDING The sharpening sequence – from first to last – goes grinding, honing and stropping. Remember, you only really need to resort to grinding if your chisel or whatever has been damaged or neglected. If your tool needs grinding, make sure you use a tool rest to maintain the correct bevel angle. A slow-moving grindstone is the safest and most foolproof way to grind a bevel. It allows you time to customise and shape the tool with little risk to your hand or the steel. If you must use a high-speed bench grinder, be careful not to overheat the steel. Quench the tool often in water and don't apply too much pressure. Of course, always wear a face shield or safety glasses.

Hold the tool flat down on the rest and adjust the shield so that your eyes are protected from sparks and fragments.

Well-maintained edge

Damaged and poorly ground edge

MAINTENANCE OF TOOLS

Angle the tool so that the primary bevel is in contact and then lift the handle slightly to achieve the cutting bevel.

When honing large blades, be careful not to slip off the edge of the sharpening stone.

66 **HONING** Honing is the post-grinding procedure of rubbing the bevel edges on a series of graded stones. The object is first to remove the deep scratches on the coarse stone, and then to polish the metal to a finer and finer finish. Again, be careful to maintain the correct bevel angle. A number of special fixtures are available to help hold the tool at the right sharpening angle. Being mindful that the honed tool is razor sharp, be sure to store it in a safe place when the job is done.

BE WARNED – in the knowledge that fine wisps of waste metal are very dangerous – they can easily pierce the skin and get in your eyes – always lubricate the stone (oil stones with honing oil and water stones with water) to hold the waste down, and maintain the stone's efficiency. Wipe up when you have finished.

67 **STROPPING** The final and finest procedure in the sharpening sequence is stropping. The purpose of the exercise is to polish the cutting edge to the shiniest of shiny finishes, and to remove the fine wisp of waste metal – the wire – that clings to the edge of the bevel. Remember, that while stropped tools are safe in use – because they get the job done swiftly and cleanly – they are also dangerous in the wrong hands. If you have children around, be sure to store the tools in a safe place.

MAINTENANCE OF TOOLS

HAMMERS If you have a hammer with a loose head or a split handle – or even an axe or adze come to that – then either get a new one, or spend time fixing it. Drive another wedge into the top of the head, or fit a replacement handle.

FILES A file with a loose handle, or no handle, is a dangerous menace – more a weapon than a woodworking tool. Some woodworkers grind old files to shape and use them for lathe tools, but be mindful that when a file shatters catastrophically, it throws out a shower of sharp-edged fragments. Never use a file without a handle. To fit a wooden handle to a file, first grip the blade in a padded vice, and then tap the handle home with a hammer or wooden mallet. Do not hit the file blade.

Never use a file without a handle.

Be sure to tap the handle onto the blade – never the other way around.

MAINTENANCE OF TOOLS

70 **RUST** Rust is a two-fold problem: It not only damages tools and machines and so consequently makes them potentially unsafe – it also stains the wood. As the underside of metal planes, and cutting blades, and the like can't be painted, many woodworkers advocate a generous dusting with baby powder/talc. The thinking is, that the powder not only displaces moisture, it also serves as a good lubricant between the wood and the tool/machine. If you keep your workshop dry and well ventilated, you shouldn't have any problems.

1. Use a fine-grade wire wool to remove rust.

2. Be mindful that when you clean the plane sole, you must use an even all-over stroke.

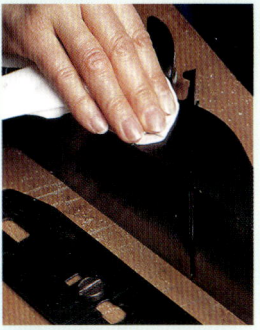

3. Protect the now clean metal with a film of fine engine oil.

71 **LUBRICATION** Lubrication needs to be near the top of your safety check list. Machine surfaces occasionally need to be wiped over with thin oil or wax, moving machine parts need to be lubricated according to the user's manual, in certain instances the undersides of metal hand planes need to be wiped over with oil or wax, and so on. If you hear squeaks and groans when you power up a machine, then the chances are it needs proper lubrication. Just remember: if a moving part is badly in need of lubrication, then it might fail catastrophically!

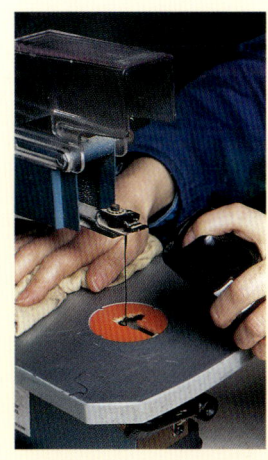

Having lubricated the moving parts – spray the work table with wax polish to achieve a low friction surface.

FINISHING

Though wood finishing can be a wonderfully satisfying activity – when you can at last see a project coming together – it is also an operation that is fraught with potential dangers, not the least of which are poisonous fumes, toxic liquids, flammable and corrosive substances. The good news is that most finishing accidents can be easily prevented simply by avoiding such sloppy workshop procedures as not reading labels and leaving adhesives, etc, just sitting around on the work surfaces. Such pitfalls can easily be side-stepped. The following tips will show you how.

SMOKING Do not smoke in the workshop. No matter how careful you are, the wood dust or shavings might catch fire, or flammable finishes might ignite, or a cigarette end might fall behind a bench, and so on. Smoking and workshops are a bad mixture! Put up NO SMOKING signs so that visitors get the message clearly.

SANDING When you come to sanding, position the dust collector or vacuum so that the hose inlet is nicely placed over the working area. For convenience, you can design a flex-arm arrangement, so that the machine can be quickly relocated.

Be aware that all wood dust is potentially toxic.

74 ALLERGIC REACTIONS

If you find yourself sneezing, or coming up with a skin rash, or your nose is running, then you need either to go for another wood type or finish or you need to reconsider your body protection arrangements. Many woodworkers opt for wearing latex gloves and disposable cover-alls.

If your power tool isn't fitted with a dust collector, then use a mobile vacuum.

FINISHING

75

FINISHES In the push towards making workshops safer, woodworkers are more and more advocating the use of non-toxic, low-odour, non-flammable water-based paints, stains and varnishes. Note that there are specific restrictions that limit the use of traditional finishes like spirit varnish. If you are employing people and are ignorant about toxic finishes and the like, then contact the DHSS or DTI and ask for advice. You should also obtain copies of Material Safety and Data Sheets (MSDS) from the manufacturers of products you use.

76

PAINTING AREA If you have it in mind to do a lot of painting, then it's best if you organise a small, clean dust-free area that is set aside for finishing. You could either screen off some part of the workshop and provide it with positive ventilation – so that air tracks from the painting area to the outside – or you could go for a totally separate room. Any fan used in a spray finishing area should be of the explosion-proof variety.

A spray gun needs to be used with great care and caution.

FINISHING

77 **TOXIC WASTE** If and when you come to dispose of toxic waste materials, like old paint, or waste motor oil, or leftovers of adhesive, or whatever, first store them outside the workshop in a clearly labelled metal bin, and then seek the advice of your local council for proper disposal. Be mindful that it's not a good idea to mix chemicals.

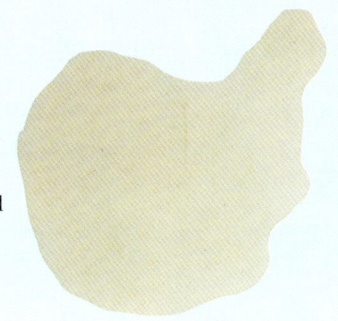

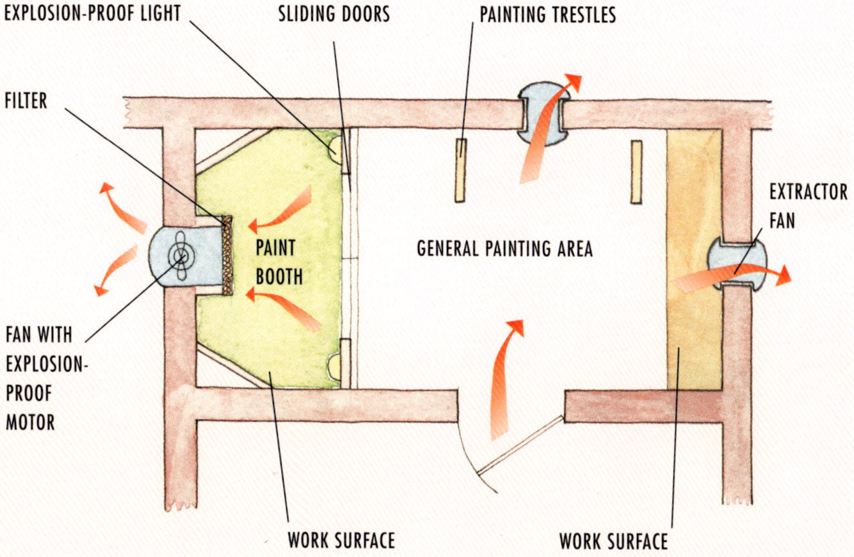

EXPLOSION-PROOF LIGHT
SLIDING DOORS
PAINTING TRESTLES
FILTER
PAINT BOOTH
GENERAL PAINTING AREA
EXTRACTOR FAN
FAN WITH EXPLOSION-PROOF MOTOR
WORK SURFACE
WORK SURFACE

Set an area aside for brush and spray painting.

WHAT TO DO IN AN EMERGENCY

Okay, so you run the cleanest, tidiest workshop in the road, and you have put every single safeguard in place. But what if? What are you going to do if there is an emergency? On the premise that it's much better to be prepared, the following guides will show you how to set up a positive emergency programme – just in case!

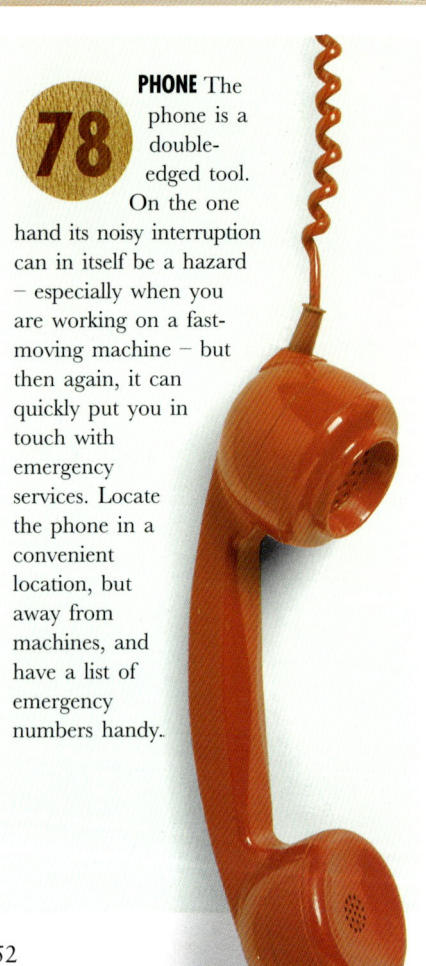

78 PHONE The phone is a double-edged tool. On the one hand its noisy interruption can in itself be a hazard – especially when you are working on a fast-moving machine – but then again, it can quickly put you in touch with emergency services. Locate the phone in a convenient location, but away from machines, and have a list of emergency numbers handy.

79 WORK PROGRAMME You don't want to be left in some sort of home-alone nightmare – bleeding, trapped on the floor, with your finger caught. That's why it's a good idea to always tell friends and family what you are doing, and just how long you intend to be in the workshop. You could have a positive policy of telling your nearest and dearest just how long you are going to be working – like a pilot tells his estimated time of arrival.

WHAT TO DO IN AN EMERGENCY

80 **EYE INJURIES** If you get something in your eye, do not rub the eye, or rub the lid over the eye, or poke around with a toothpick or use an eye cup. Simply hold a sterile dressing over the closed eye with a plaster, and immediately go to the nearest casualty department. DO NOT DRIVE – get a friend or helper to do the driving or phone for an ambulance.

81 **CUTS AND SPLINTERS** If you have a workshop, then its only a matter of time before you scrape a knuckle, or cut your finger on a chisel, or run a splinter up your fingernail or whatever. It's a good idea to be ready with a well-stocked first aid kit. You need bandages, gauze, a pair of scissors, a pair of tweezers, a sterilised needle, and a tube/bottle of antiseptic to rub on the wound.

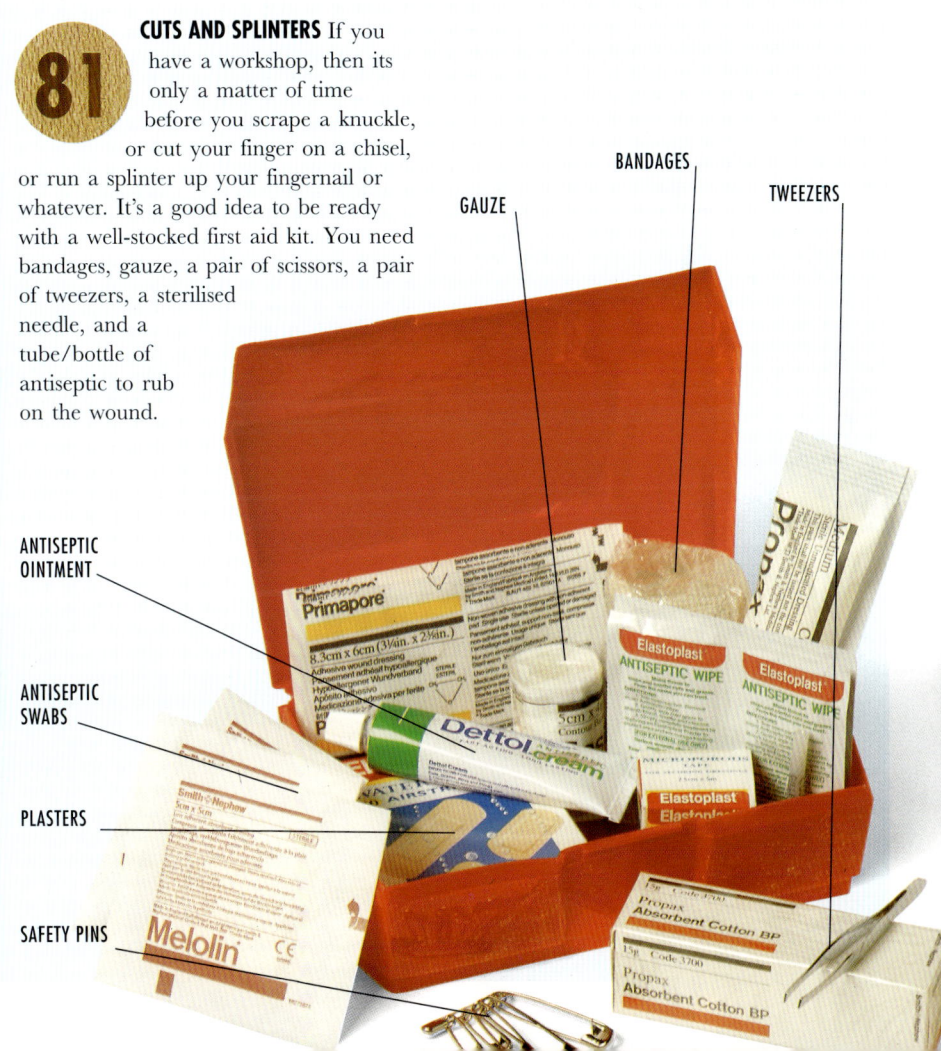

WHAT TO DO IN AN EMERGENCY

82 **FIRST AID CHART** An accident like a nasty gash to the hand or a crushed finger is not uncommon in the workshop. This being the case, you should display a basic first aid chart on the wall, familiarise yourself with recommended first aid practices and list the emergency phone numbers of your doctor or hospital casualty department.

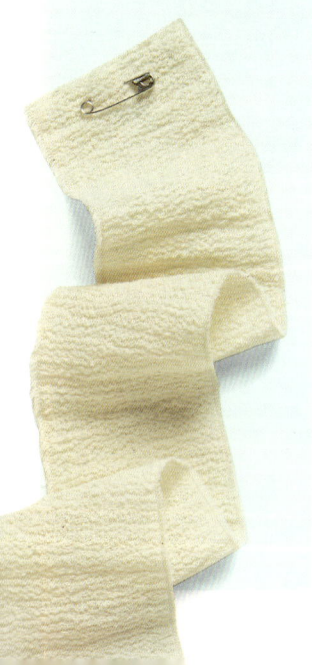

FIRE EXTINGUISHERS   FIRE BLANKET   FIRE CHART
WATER   SAND

Make sure that your fire extinguishers are in good condition and easy to reach.

83 **FIRE EXTINGUISHERS** Every workshop should have at least one fire extinguisher of the dry powder type, a bucket of water, a bucket of sand and a fire blanket. In an emergency, like, say, an electrical glue pot bursting into flame, you should first of all turn off the power, and then control the fire with the sand and/or the extinguisher. On no account should you start throwing the water around onto live machinery. For even more protection, position extinguishers at different points around the shop.

Check that your extinguishers can be used on electrical fires.

WHAT TO DO IN AN EMERGENCY

84 **EMERGENCY EXITS** Your workshop must have, at the very least, two exits – say an unobstructed door, and a large opening window. If you are working upstairs, then you also need to plan a suitable fire escape. If you are employing help – even on a part-time basis – then you must follow recommended guidelines. If you have any doubts, seek the advice of your local health and safety officer.

Clean the dust and dirt from the inside of the smoke alarm.

85 **SMOKE ALARMS** If you are anxious about fire risks – and this is perhaps more of a problem if your workshop is an integral part of your home – then smoke alarms are a must. They are a swift, sure, money-saving means of detecting smoke. The average large-garage size workshop should have three alarms – one at the centre of the room, one farthest away from the door and one nearest the door.

WHAT TO DO IN AN EMERGENCY

86 **SEVERED FINGERS** Okay, so it's not a pleasant notion – but it is a possibility, and accidents do happen! A current magazine article tells how, when a woodworker cut three of his fingers off on the band saw, he bound his hand up with a towel to stop the blood, packed the fingers in a box with frozen fish sticks and then drove to the hospital where the fingers were successfully sewn back on. Apparently, what saved the fingers was the fact that they were frozen. Just remember: Frozen fingers are better than no fingers!

87 **ELECTRICAL SHOCK** In case of electrical shock – when the accident victim is holding the cable, tool or whatever – the first thing to do is to turn off the power. This should be swiftly followed up with a phone call to the emergency services, wrapping the victim up in a blanket and making sure the mouth is clear of obstructions.

BE WARNED – resuscitation techniques need to be done with care and caution. Follow the advice as shown on your emergency chart.

If your power tool looks like this little beauty – a ragged flex and bits of tape – then switch off the power and have the tool overhauled.

88 **SEVERE BLEEDING** When arteries are cut or a number of veins have been lacerated, severe bleeding will occur – usually in bright red spurts. The first aid provider – this might even be the victim himself/herself – should immediately locate the source of the pumping blood, and then apply finger pressure or whole-hand pressure with a sterile gauze or towel to stop the flow.

SPECIFIC MACHINE TOOL SAFETY

Not so long ago, the average small workshop had a table saw, maybe a drill press and a router, and that was about it. All the other tasks were performed with hand tools. Now of course, most woodshops are chock-a-block with all manner of powerful fast-running efficient machines – everything from lathes, band saws, planers, jointers, power carvers and scroll saws, through to bench saws, chain saws, shapers and sanders. There's no denying that machines pose the biggest safety problems, if only because, when machine accidents do occur, they tend to be swift and catastrophic. The best overall advice – having first read the user manual – is never to work on a machine until you have a clear understanding as to its function, and to always keep machines well maintained. The following machine-specific tips will help you run a safe and efficient workshop.

If your workpiece is short, then be sure to use push sticks. Never put your hands at risk.

89

TABLE SAW If you intend to rip a long length on a table saw, you must use the machine in conjunction with an outfeed table and hold-downs. The outfeed table minimises problems involved with wood kickback and binding, and the hold-down stops the workpiece from rising off the worktable to the point where it is thrown back like a javelin. Always wear safety glasses, always use push sticks, and always make sure that the push-sticks stay away from the blades. Not forgetting that, if the wood chatters and starts to split, then it might split off and shoot backwards like a spear. Always stand well to one side of the line of feed.

SPECIFIC MACHINE TOOL SAFETY

PORTABLE PLANER

90 A portable planer is a wonderfully efficient tool – perfect for the small workshop. Having protected yourself against the dust and the noise, the main hazards have to do with feed and kick-back. The primary rules are: never try to plane a piece shorter than about 30cm (12 inches), never stand directly behind the machine, never force the rate of feed and never let small children anywhere near when the machine is up and running.

1. When working with a long length of wood, use your hands to start the cut.

91 BAND SAW Though the band saw is one of the most efficient woodworking machines going, its very efficiency tends to lull the woodworker into thinking that it can be used with careless abandon – like a food mixer. No way! A current magazine likens the band saw to a quiet beast that is just waiting to nip your fingers off. The good news is that bird's-mouth push sticks can be swiftly and easily made in just a few minutes – a great money-saving safety aid! In use, the push sticks are held like cutlery, and used to feed and guide the workpiece through the machine. Always lower the upper blade guide so as little of the blade is exposed as possible.

SPECIFIC MACHINE TOOL SAFETY

Scroll saws are uniquely safe – perfect for anxious beginners.

92 **SCROLL SAW** If you are a nervous beginner to woodwork, and you have it in mind to cut fancy curves and profiles in thin wood – say hand-size pieces up to 3cm (1¼ inches) thick – then the scroll saw is the machine for you. This machine is just about as safe and foolproof as you can get. Its uniquely high safety record is borne out by the fact that the scroll saw is one of the few woodworking machines allowed in schools for young kids.

2. When the end of the workpiece comes to within 15cm (6 inches) of the blade, use a pair of push sticks.

3. When you come to finish, reduce the rate of cut, and reposition the push sticks for optimum control.

SPECIFIC MACHINE SAFETY

Use a brush, cloth and white spirit to clean away the build-up of resin. The shanks need to be bright and free from pits and steel-burn.

93 ROUTER A router is a great tool for cutting slots and profiles, and for producing mouldings – a real must for the small workshop. The main accidents and mess-ups with the router have to do with leaving the bit in place, and with not cleaning up the dust and resin once the job is done. The gradual build-up results in wear and bit slippage. Don't be tempted to polish the shank or the collet with wire wool, as repeated cleanings will make for a loose and sloppy fit. Simply wipe it with white spirit and a thin smear of light oil.

94 LATHE If and when you find that you need a lathe, get yourself the biggest and best that you can afford. In use, the lathe is a relatively safe and user-friendly machine, as long as you follow a few rules. Always make sure that your clothes and hair are tied back before you switch on the power. Always work with long-handled tools. And always make sure that the workpiece is totally secure. As the most common accidents have to do with the workpiece flying off, you must always wear goggles, or better yet, an all-over face visor-respirator. If you are really nervous, you could fit a safety shield in front of the machine.

Aim for a lathe that has big, bold, positive stay-put controls and a heavy vibration-free structure.

SPECIFIC MACHINE SAFETY

A selection of router cutters that have seen a lot of hard use. These can be cleaned up and honed by hand or completely re-sharpened.

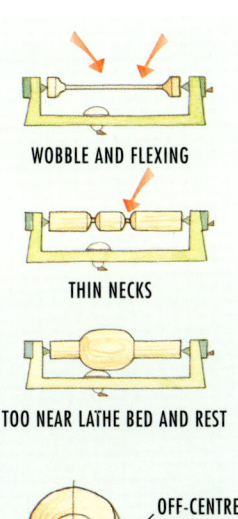

WOBBLE AND FLEXING

THIN NECKS

TOO NEAR LATHE BED AND REST

OFF-CENTRE DAMAGES BEARINGS

95 **PLATE JOINTER** A portable plate or biscuit jointer is a good tool – a valuable addition to most workshops. In essence, it cuts slots or kerfs in such a way that mating pieces of wood can be butted and joined together by means of a thin plate of compressed wood called a biscuit. In use, accidents have to do with the workpiece shifting, and/or the tool bucking. The two primary safety points to stay with are to spend plenty of time securing the workpiece and to make sure that the anti-kickback pins are in contact with the wood to be slotted.

Biscuit joint insert

SPECIFIC MACHINE SAFETY

BAND SAW BLADES
96 When you buy a new band saw blade, it will be tightly coiled up on itself – a bit like a spring. Being mindful that it will bounce open the moment you undo the binding – a whole hoop of razor sharp teeth – the best procedure is to wear gloves and a face mask. Then unwrap the blade in an open area by tossing it out away from you on the floor, where it can harmlessly spring back to its natural shape.

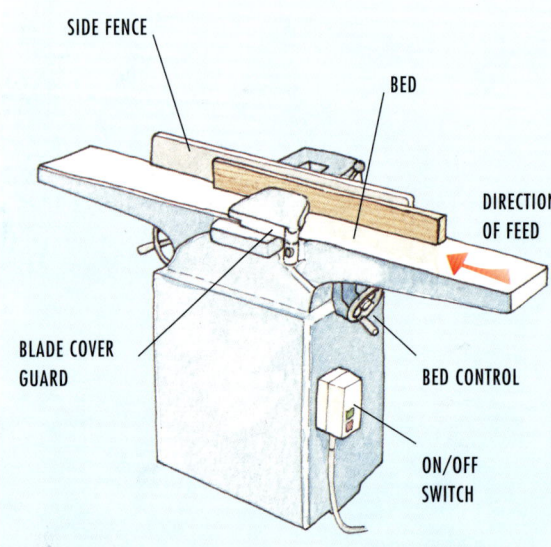

A small combination planer-jointer

97 SURFACE PLANER The surface planer is the fastest and most accurate way to achieve truly square sides and edges on your timber, but the planer is also one of the most dangerous machines in the woodshop. Always keep guards in place and be careful to keep fingers away from the cutterhead. Use push sticks and push blocks to guide the work past the cutterhead. Do not plane pieces shorter than 30cm (12 inches).

SPECIFIC MACHINE SAFETY

98 **DRILL PRESS** Although the bench drill press has a pretty good safety record, the fact that it is used at chest and face level does put you at special risk. Long hair, loose clothing or jewellery are all a hazard. The drill press's small table also presents a problem when drilling large workpieces. Make sure large pieces are properly supported and clamped.

If you are working with a drill bit larger than 1cm (½ inch) diameter, then be sure to hold the workpiece in a clamp or vice.

99 **MACHINE MOMENTUM** Most woodworking machines carry on moving even after switch-off, so you mustn't be tempted to stop the blade or chuck with your hands. Use a length of scrap wood instead.

100 **MACHINE LOCATION** A really good money-saving tip for securing machines and benches to the floor – so that they stay put, don't wobble and are safe – is first to wedge them to the correct height with thin shims of wood, then use a glue gun to run a bead around the base of the machine. When the glue is set, the little ridge will prevent the wedges from slipping out, and so prevent the machine from creeping.

CREDITS

Quarto Publishing would like to thank the following for their permission to reproduce copyright material: p6 Ercol Furniture, Buckinghamshire; p26 Image Bank.

All other photographs are the copyright of Quarto Publishing.

We would like to acknowledge and thank Axminster Power Tool Centre, Chard Street, Axminster, Devon, who very kindly loaned the tools and equipment featured in this book.

We would finally like to thank Tim Hodgkinson, Simone Oliver and Alan Thomas at Pendryn Furniture, 2b Barbican Industrial Estate, East Looe, Cornwall, who kindly permitted us to photograph at their premises.

Senior Art editor Penny Cobb
Designer Glyn Bridgewater
Photographers Ian Howes, Jeremy Thomas
Illustrator Gill Bridgewater
Text editor William Sampson
Senior editor Kate Kirby
Prop researcher Miriam Hyman
Picture manager Giulia Hetherington
Editorial director Mark Dartford
Art director Moira Clinch

Typeset by Genesis Typesetting, Rochester and
Central Southern Typesetters, Eastbourne
Manufactured by Bright Arts (Singapore) Pte Ltd.
Printed in China by Leefung-Asco Printers Ltd.